AFRICA:
TROUBLED CONTINENT

[A Problems Approach]

By

Harry A. Gailey
San Jose State University

ROBERT E. KRIEGER PUBLISHING COMPANY, INC.
MALABAR, FLORIDA
1983

Original Edition 1983

Printed and Published by
ROBERT E. KRIEGER PUBLISHING COMPANY, INC.
KRIEGER DRIVE
MALABAR, FLORIDA 32950

Copyright © 1983 by
ROBERT E. KRIEGER PUBLISHING COMPANY, INC.

Printed in the United States of America

Library of Congress Cataloging in Publication Data

Gailey, Harry A.
  Africa, troubled continent—a problems approach.

  Bibliography: p.
  1. Africa—Politics and government—1960–
2. Africa—Economic conditions—1960–   . 3. Africa—
Social conditions—1960–   . I. Title.
DT30.5.G335   1983   960'.32   82-23342
ISBN 0-89874-342-7

for

MELANIE JOY

and

MICHELLE

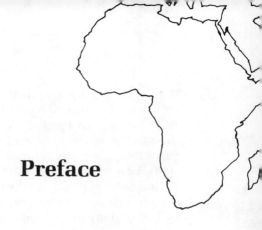

Preface

Writing a book which focused upon the major problems of Africa had never occurred to me although I had long been aware that no such introductory work for the general reader had been attempted. I therefore was very hesitant about undertaking such a project after it was suggested that I construct an African "problems" book. One reason was the obvious fact that no one can know enough about the huge, complex continent to feel secure even in merely describing the oftentimes confusing flow of events. To deal with African problems demands not only factual knowledge but a control of a process of synthesis which applied to each state or territory would indicate whether a specific problem was unique or typical. Another reason for my hesitation was a desire to continue in the role of the unattached and relatively unaffected observer of events. In all my other books and articles I had tried not to intrude any more than necessary, letting the story develop with a minimal amount of extraneous comment from me.

The project continued to intrigue me, and finally, contrary to all the reasons just cited, I decided to try to provide a "problems" book. Although the choice of problems was mine, I believe that anyone familiar with the continent would concur in most of my choices. I have foregone footnoting, one defense utilized by most scholars, myself included, believing that this would detract from the narrative flow. However, I have provided a lengthy Bibliography for those readers who wish to pursue further any of the problems only alluded to in this short work. This book is a personal statement as much as a recounting of failed promises, broken hopes, misery, and death which has been the lot of so many Africans during the past quarter-century. I do not attempt to hide my revulsion for certain political and economic developments which have contributed to the growing frustrations of millions of Africans. Neither do I wish to disguise my feelings of hopelessness in the face of burgeoning populations, increasing dessication of the land, and the wanton slaughter of Africa's irreplaceable, precious wildlife. I do not ask that the reader agree with each of my analyses or conclusions, but that he read this as an honest attempt by an Africanist to present a range of the most serious problems to the educated, concerned reader. Any dialogue is better than the silence which partially by inadvertence and partly by design now obscures many of these subjects. Myths and wishful thinking may have their place, but they are poor points of departure if the many near desperate problems of the continent are ever to be solved.

Harry A. Gailey
August 1981

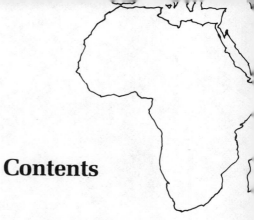

Contents

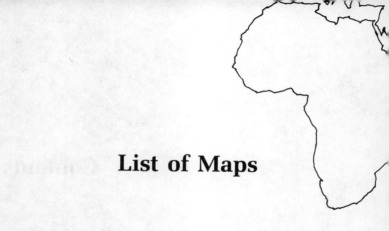

List of Maps

ONE

Geographic Realities

Any analysis of Africa's general problems must begin with those environmental factors which directly affect human life and development but are only slightly amenable to alteration by man. The most important of these are size, land forms, climate, and quality of soil. Each of these establishes certain limits to man's endeavors and restricts what any cultural system can achieve. At best, Africa's geography is a challenge to its political leaders. At worst, conditions in many regions of the huge continent present insuperable barriers to gaining even a minimal portion of the legitimate goals for the improvement of the life of the people.

In the past two decades new myths about Africa have been created to replace many of the discredited concepts of an earlier age. One of the most pervasive of these concerns the unity of Africa. Whether applied to peoples, politics, or geography, this idea leads many persons in the Western world to discount diversity and treat Africa as if it were a single entity. Such a premise is most damaging in the political sphere, but it also leads to erroneous assumptions even in the most obvious areas of analysis such as Africa's size. Thus one of the first facts which must be stressed about Africa is its overwhelming size.

Africa is not a country, but a continent—the second largest in the world—with an area of 11.7 million square miles. It extends almost an equal distance north and south of the equator. The extreme north-south distance is almost five thousand miles. The continent is wider in the northern hemisphere with a maximum width almost that of the north-south distance. Two-thirds of Africa's land mass lies in the northern hemisphere with approximately 9 million square miles falling within the tropic zone. These vast distances and the correlate problems posed can best be illustrated by a few comparisons. If superimposed over northern Africa, the United States would fit neatly into the Sahara Desert. Two more duplicates of the United States would be necessary to cover the rest of the continent. A final example of differential size should suffice. If one places the map of Africa over the western hemisphere with Cape Town at the same latitude as Buenos Aires, then Tunis would be located in the vicinity of Atlanta, Georgia.

Glancing at a map, one of the first impressions one has of Africa is the length of its relatively unbroken coastline. In the north the Mediterranean coast is almost 2,300 miles long and the coastline of the Red Sea is over 1,600 miles. There are no deep gulfs to intrude on the continental mass of Africa. Except for the connection with Asia Minor at the Sinai Peninsula, Africa is totally separate from any other land mass. Even this land bridge was penetrated by the Suez Canal in 1869, and today the hundred-mile length of the canal effectively divides the continents. The narrow Straits of Gibraltar at the western end of the Mediterranean separates Africa from Europe. The Straits of Bab-el-Mandeb at the southern end of the Red Sea provides a twenty-mile gulf between Africa and Arabia.

There are few rocky headlands which shelter bays. Most of these are located in either the extreme north or south. In those places there are excellent harbors such as Bizerte, Cape Town, Durban, and Maputo (Lourenço Marques). Few African rivers have estuaries which could also provide natural harbors. Rather, the norm is either a large, swampy mangrove-overgrown delta such as the Niger or Zambesi, or rivers whose outlets are blocked by sandbars as with the Calabar, Cross, or Orange Rivers. Along the coastline of West Africa the desert and in some cases the forest come down almost to the ocean and large, beautiful sandy beaches are formed. The offshore currents can create sandy islands which lie a few miles from the coastline. The intervening narrow channels block direct access to the ocean. In some places, such as at Abidjan or Lagos, these islands are breached and the lagoons, with deepening, become excellent harbors. Despite the presence of a few good natural harbors in the west such as at Banjul and Freetown and at Dar-es-Salaam in the east, the most salient fact of the African coast is its lack of harbors. This has meant that in order to ensure adequate development, African coastal states have had to expend great sums of money in the construction of ports. There is no better example of this than Ghana which had no natural port capable of taking even moderate-sized ocean-going ships at the time of its independence in 1957.

The continental shelf of Africa, except for the Mediterranean and Red Sea areas, is quite narrow. Normally the gently sloping shelf extends only a short distance from shore before falling off to depths of upwards of 2,000 fathoms. The narrowness of the shelf has had great effect upon the climate of the adjacent land, particularly in northwest and southwest Africa. Since there is little warm shallow water, most of the currents are very cold, and with the prevalent winds being offshore, this has meant only a small amount of rainfall. The lands adjacent to the cold currents, the western Sahara and the Namib, are arid in the extreme. The narrowness of the shelf also has a limiting role to play in Africa's economic future. In the past quarter-century, large petroleum deposits have been discovered under these sandy sloping shelves. Already offshore drilling has been important for Nigeria. However, with few continental sedimentary beds, the lack of a wide shelf is another limiting factor for African development.

The most prominent land form in northern Africa is the Sahara Desert which presents a highly diverse topography. Much of its surface is rocky, and there are three large highlands located in the central portion. Dried-out river beds or wadis crisscross the desert, particularly numerous near the highlands. Only the ergs are composed of shifting sand, and a number of regions are made up entirely of these large interconnected complexes of sand dunes. The sandy ergs are particularly numerous in the extreme western Sahara.

There are other smaller desert areas in Africa. Much of Somalia and eastern Ethiopia is desert as is the northern section of Kenya. However, the continent's second largest desert is the Kalahari which occupies more than 225,000 square miles and covers the bulk of South-West Africa (Namibia), the northwestern part of the Republic of South Africa, and western Botswana. As is the case of the Sahara, the land forms of the Kalahari area vary from the sand swept dunes of the Namib, to the highlands near Windhoek, to the rocky soil of the main portion of the central desert. The one common factor in all the desert regions, that which in fact makes them a desert, is the low incidence of rainfall varying from no annual precipitation to a maximum of ten inches a year.

Despite modern technological advances, the deserts can support only small specialized populations, and they remain as in the past a barrier to trade and communication between peoples and cultures. Desert peoples, whether Tuareg, Danakil, Somali, or Khoi, are generally migratory, earning their livelihood by trading, raiding, or keeping herds of goats or camels. The Sahara which has blocked easy interior communication from the more technically advanced Mediterranean has, nevertheless, well-established trading routes. These have been known and exploited for over 1,500 years. Such long-distance travel in a hostile environment was made possible by the development of oases cultures where the presence of water made it possible for a significant population to exist in the midst of the desert. Until the twentieth century these date-producing, resupply centers remained an important part of the economic life of West and North Africa. Watering places were also important for the inhabitants of the other desert regions of Africa, but no similar centers of trade developed in the deserts of the Horn and southern Africa.

Immediately adjacent to the desert regions are the grasslands, the most typical of all of Africa's features. This savannah land is largely defined by the amount of rainfall which varies between 10 and 20 inches annually and is seasonal. In the areas of least rainfall the soil is more sandy and the coarse grasses are scattered and bunched. Acacia and other thorn trees are very sparse in this zone. In the northern hemisphere this more arid part of the savannah has been called the Sahel. With normal rainfall these grasslands could support a significant human population who kept herds of cattle, goats, and camels. By following well-established, centuries-old paths of movement within a region, sufficient amounts of grass and water could be found. However, the growth of human and animal populations in the twentieth century combined with mismanagement of the lands nearest the desert proper has resulted in a steady advance of the desert and a subsequent lessening of the ability of the Sahel to support life. The disastrous drought years of the decade after 1965 resulted in the deaths of hundreds of thousands of people, the destruction of most of their domestic animals, and the ending of a way of life for many pastoral peoples in the broad savannah zone stretching from Senegal to Ethiopia.

The savannah areas which normally receive more than 20 inches of rain annually have a larger variety of grasses, bushes, and trees. Grain agriculture as well as pastoralism has been a feature of these regions. A variety of millets, wheat, and in recent years export crops such as peanuts and cotton do well in this zone. Phasing into the grasslands in East and Central Africa are the savannah forests where one finds more and larger trees although not of such size and quality to be valuable for timber. The grasslands and adjacent savannah forests traditionally supported the largest human population of the continent. Most of the inhabitants were clan or tribal oriented people and well into the twentieth century their cultures based on subsistance agriculture were relatively undisturbed. The grasslands and scrub forest regions were also the homeland for the vast herds of wildlife which until a generation ago were such a marked feature of subequatorial Africa.

Much of Africa is an uplifted plateau which is over 7,000 feet high in the south, sloping gradually downward as one moves northward. Except for the Atlas ranges in the north and the Drakensberg Mountains in South Africa, this high plateau is bordered by narrow low-lying coastal plains. The escarpment between the high plateau and the coasts can be very dramatic as in Natal, but generally there is a gradual progression from the plateau to the lowlands. There has been little folding of the basic rock of the African continent. The plateau has rather been created by a dramatic upward movement caused by the earth's internal pressures.

This upward movement which occurred approximately 25 million years ago had a number of interrelated effects on the topography of Africa. During the uplift, the solid block of the eastern part of the continent cracked. The resultant fractures follow roughly a line from the coast of the Red Sea southwestward to the borders of the Republic of South Africa. Along these fracture lines the plateau was displaced downward to form troughs or rifts which vary in width from a few hundred yards to many miles. The rift lines, particularly in East Africa, are very complex but there are essentially two distinct rifts. The main stem of the rift branches into western and eastern rifts at Lake Turkana (Rudolf) which combine into a single major rift again north of Lake Tanganyika.

The period of uplift and cracking was accompanied by considerable volcanic activity. Vast areas of southern Ethiopia and northern Kenya were covered by lava flows and volcanic ash. The great highlands of eastern Africa were also created at this time. Most of the high mountains peaks such as Kilimanjaro, Kenya, Ruwenzori, Meru, and Elgon are all volcanic cones dating from the same period. Another result of the geologic shifts was the formation of large bodies of water. These have largely disappeared, leaving behind sedimentary deposits such as those in the Upper Niger and Lake Chad regions. The present-day lakes of East Africa are a reminder of this period because parts of the troughs

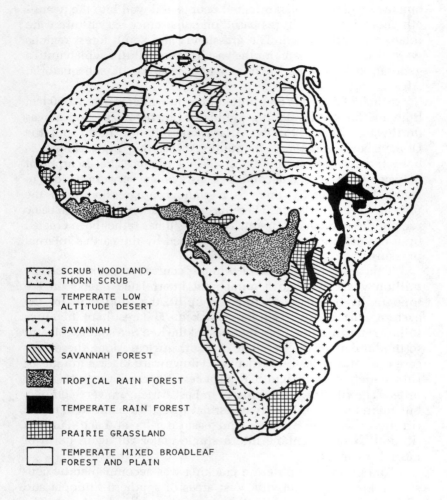

SCRUB WOODLAND,
THORN SCRUB

TEMPERATE LOW
ALTITUDE DESERT

SAVANNAH

SAVANNAH FOREST

TROPICAL RAIN FOREST

TEMPERATE RAIN FOREST

PRAIRIE GRASSLAND

TEMPERATE MIXED BROADLEAF
FOREST AND PLAIN

Generalized Vegetation Pattern

created by the cracking of the earth were filled with water. The great lakes of Africa including Turkana, Albert (Mobutu), Edward, Kivu, Tanganyika, and Malawi are all located in the rift zone as is Lake Victoria, the world's third largest lake.

Volcanic activity was less intense in West Africa and more localized. There are, therefore, fewer highlands in this vast region. The Cameroon and Adamawa Highlands anchored in the south by Mount Cameroon, the highest mountain in western Africa, are the best examples of uplift, lava flow, and faulting. The Futa Jallon, the source of West Africa's major rivers, located in modern day Guinea and Sierra Leone, is another region created by the earth's upward movement. The Ahaggar and Tibesti Highlands situated in the Sahara Desert are remnants of two distinct periods of earth movement which created very extensive mountains. The present-day highlands, still vast in extent with individual peaks ranging over 10,000 feet in elevation, are all that is left of the old mountains after weathering over the millenia.

The most recent mountains in Africa are the Atlas ranges which separate the fertile Mediterranean coastal plain of northern Africa from the Sahara Desert. The Atlas Mountains were created by the same geologic forces which formed the mountains of Europe and show evidence of considerable folding. Some experts believe that there was a northward shifting of the earth mass of Africa at this time causing the uplift and folding of the European alpine ranges. The only mountains in Africa which evidence a similar form of folding to those found in Europe are the Atlas.

An old stereotype of Africa was that of "the jungle." Generations of people nurtured by the fertile imagination of Edgar Rice Burroughs came to believe that sub-Saharan Africa was largely an area of tropical rain forest. On the contrary, less than 9 percent of the total area comprises forest lands. Temperate rain forests located mainly in the higher elevations of eastern Africa and Ethiopia make up only a very small portion of Africa's forests. More widespread are the lowland tropical rain forests. There is a narrow tropical rain forest belt, varying in width from 50 to 200 miles, which lies adjacent to the west coast of Africa and extends from the Gambia River to the southern border of the Cameroons. This belt merges with the tropical forests of the Congo basin which contain by far the most extensive tropical forests in Africa. Rainfall and temperatures are high in the forest lands and this combination provides luxuriant undergrowth and trees of many varieties which are in some cases over 100 feet high. Many of these trees have great economic value. Varieties of rosewood, ebony, and mahogany provide the Ivory Coast, Niger, the Cameroons, Gabon, and Zaire with a valued export-oriented timber industry. There is a heavy concentration of oil palm in Nigeria, the Cameroons, and parts of Central Africa. Other rattan and raphia palms grow wild throughout this region, providing materials for local use in building and in profitable craft industries. A considerable portion of the equatorial forest zone is swamp forest, generally concentrated along the banks of the major rivers but particularly abundant in the delta lands. The dominant type of tree in these locales is some type of mangrove, varieties of which reach heights of over 50 feet. The mangrove is so well-adapted to its hostile watery environment that the intrusion of salt water does not kill the plant. In parts of West Africa the roots of saline mangrove trees are a valuable source of salt for the local people and were at one time an important trading item.

The forests of Africa are in danger, however. The tremendous growth of the human population in certain areas has increased the need for building materials and firewood. Observers have noted particularly the rapid deforestation of lands in the Atlas areas of North Africa, parts of Kenya and Uganda, Zaire, Zambia, and Lesotho. Until recently the cutting of trees for local use as well as for export has gone on relatively unchecked even in those states such as the Ivory Coast and Gabon with well-developed timber industries. In the past decade some of the affluent states with more progressive leadership such as Ivory Coast, Kenya, and Gabon have begun programs designed to limit cutting and provide for reforestation. It is too soon to say whether even in such states the programs will be enough to reverse the trend toward unlimited cutting which could exhaust the export timber resources in only a few decades.

The last set of features which should be considered in this brief geographic survey are the rivers and basins of Africa. Despite its deserved reputation for heat and dryness, Africa is the home of hundreds of rivers. An aerial view of parts of West and Central Africa shows a maze of streams and mangrove-clotted deltas of dozens of streams flowing into the ocean. Some of the world's greatest rivers are found in Africa. Many rivers such as the Gambia, Rokel, Ogun, Cross, Cuenene, Kasai, and Tana, considered by African standards to be secondary streams, would be great rivers if located elsewhere. They are, however, dwarfed by comparison to the magnificent Niger, Congo, Zambesi, Orange,

Limpopo, or Nile systems. These six great rivers drain two-thirds of the surface of Africa.

However different are these major rivers, they tend to have certain common elements which have in the past restricted their usefulness. Very few are navigable for any great distances inland. Most of the West African rivers have bars near their mouths which preclude entrance of large ships into the main part of the river. The greatest river system in Africa, that of the Congo Basin, is similarly restricted because the rapids of Malebo (Stanley) Pool, 250 miles up the Congo River, block the use of the river until one reaches the vicinity of Kinshasa. From there the Congo is navigable for major ships for over 1,000 miles into the interior of Zaire. There are exceptions to the stricture about the marginal use of African rivers as means of easy, cheap transportation and communication. Many of the adjunct rivers of the Congo such as the Lualaba, Ubangi, Kwango, and Kasai are useful as means of transport. The Niger River is usable by commercial vessels from its mouth, through the channels of the Nun and Benin Rivers, until one reaches the confluence of the Benue River near the town of Lokoja, and the White Nile is usable for great distances in the central part of Sudan and throughout its length in Egypt.

While African rivers in the past may have been underutilized, there are indications that individual governments are beginning to realize that they are an unrecognized major resource. Most of the rivers and creeks teem with fish. In protein-poor Africa, fishing is an industry which was ignored by the bulk of the people, even those who lived adjacent to water. Now with financial aid from the central authorities, there are signs in many parts of the continent of the beginnings of potentially valuable fishing industries. During the colonial period only a few dams and irrigation systems were constructed. However, these few such as those on the Nile in Egypt and the Gezira project supporting cotton cultivation in the Sudan showed the potential of large-scale irrigation schemes. Since 1950 large dams have been constructed at Aswan in Egypt, Cabora Basa in Mozambique, Kariba in Zimbabwe, Kainji in Nigeria, Akisombo in Ghana, the Verwoerd and a variety of smaller dams on South Africa's Orange River. Each of these dams provides not only the possibility for storage of vast amounts of water for irrigation, but also electric power for the growing industrial and domestic demands of the major cities of these particular regions.

The quality of the land in all societies has a major if unheralded role in determining the kinds of culture which will be developed. In all the world's areas where agriculture is the prime occupation, the productivity of the soil becomes crucial to the life or death of each individual within a particular society. Most of Africa's peoples are still concerned with sedentary, village-based agriculture. Each traditional group whether village, clan, or tribe has evolved very distinct, prescribed ways of parceling out land, cultivating it, deciding on which crops to plant and to havest, and distributing crops. African agriculturists are generally very conservative, tending to reject much that is presented to them by Western-educated experts whether foreigners or Africans representing their own agriculture departments. There is good reason for the villagers' skepticism and conservatism. They have been taught and have observed how poor the land is and have come to a compromise with this reality. The most fundamental fact of Africa is that with rare exceptions the soils, no matter where they are found, are very poor. If the land is not treated with respect people die. One of the major tragedies of Africa is that in many regions, traditional agricultural methods instead of protecting the land are hastening its destruction.

Any analysis of the soils of Africa tends immediately to become complex since each type of soil is the result of five interrelated factors—the parent rock, climate, slope, organic matter, and age. Thus in any subregion of the continent there will be a wide variety of soils. The number of types of soil in Africa will depend upon the categories of differentiation. However, there will be at the very least forty different types of soil identified. Without going into the full complexity of soil analysis, there are some factors which must be borne in mind in any discussion of Africa's land. Parent rock with high iron content will produce what is called lateritic soil which is usually low in fertility. A quick glance at any soil map of Africa will show that a high percentage of the land south of the Sahara is lateritic. The best soils are generally uncompressed sediments in which there is a great amount of organic material. Except for the narrow coastal strip north of the Atlas Mountains, in the southern hemisphere south of the Drakensberg, and in some selected locations in the highlands, there is very little of the best type of sedimentary soils.

In terms of area, the desert soils are the most prevalent. The profile of desert soils will vary with location but they are all shallow, light-colored, and possess little organic matter. Desert topography varies from shifting sand to rocky substrata with a very thin top layer of soil. Underlying much of the desert lands is calcrete or silcrete. Water seepage and evaporation have left widespread calcium and salt deposits throughout the Sahara which make the land useless. Salt gathered from such areas, however, has been a major trading commodity for inhabitants of the Sahara for more than a thousand years.

In some desert regions such as the northern part of the Algerian Sahara, there is considerable water held close to the surface by layers of limestone. Artesian wells are even found in certain sections of this region. Some plants such as the date palm grow well in these watered sandy soils as they do in the important oases of the central Sahara. In the southernmost part of the Sahara and parts of the eastern Kalahari where rainfall is more plentiful one finds more organic material in the generally gray colored soils. These soils are also found on the desert borders in the Sahel and support the rough grasses so necessary to maintain the animal herds of local nomads. Many observers have erroneously viewed the vast desert areas as having great agricultural potential if only enough water could be found to irrigate these regions. While some sections of the desert could be made more fertile and the production of specialized products could be increased, it is doubtful that the deserts will ever become major agricultural areas. This is because of the lack of significant amounts of organic matter in most of the desert soils.

Relatively fertile chestnut or brown colored soils are located most often in the savannah zones. Normally because of the definite wet-dry seasons, these soils are leached and acid. Many of these light brown soils in western Africa respond well to chemical fertilizers and it is in such regions that peanut cultivation has provided a major export crop. Various types of rough grasses are common to the chestnut colored soil regions and these have in the past supported a significant nomadic population and their herds of goats, sheep, and cattle. Systematic use of chemical fertilizers combined with irrigation could make these chestnut and brown soils far more productive than at present.

Most of the areas north of the Congo Basin and west of the East African highlands where the rainfall is between 30 to 50 inches annually have ferruginous soils. This simply means that there is a high concentration of iron in the soil. These soils are red in color but the color alone does not indicate the soil's potential. Some of these soils are not lateritic and are well drained and nonacid. With due care, appropriate fertilizing, and allowing the land to recover during fallow periods, most of the red soils are quite productive. In addition to providing the crops needed to sustain a local population, the red soils are good for growing such export crops as sugar cane, sisal, and rubber. Some of the red soils have turned into laterite. True laterite is really not a soil but rock which has been formed by chemical action with the parent rock base. Lateritic soils can vary in productivity from the very low level of lands where there is only local encrustations of iron or alumina to solid rock plates where nothing will grow.

In humid areas of the tropical rain forests the soils also have a very heavy concentration of iron or aluminum. Lush vegetation in regions such as Gabon, Zaire, or the Congo gives the misleading impression of fertility. The apparent richness of these lands reflect only the subtle balance of nature. The detritus from the plants provides only enough organic material to support these same plants. The great amounts of rainfall preclude a build-up of a thick humus bed that one might imagine from the amounts of falling debris. Most of the nutrients are simply carried downward by the heavy flow of water. This leaves only a thin layer of topsoil covering yellow or red soils sometimes several feet thick. These are, however, heavily leached and have little organic content. Experiments in clearing the forests and undergrowth and planting normal crops have universally been unsuccessful. Denied the nutrient reinforcement of the forest detritus, the land reverts to the low productivity of the secondary layer of leached soil.

Climate has ramifications for life second only to that of the land forms of a given region. Thus in order to understand Africa's problems and potentials one should have some general knowledge of the meterological factors which influence climate. Among these are the ocean currents which so effect the weather over the land. Along the northwestern coast of Africa is found the southward-moving cold Canary current. Duplicating this along the western coast in the southern hemisphere is the northward-flowing Benguela current. These currents normally combine with the prevalent offshore winds to deny rain to the adjacent lands. Therefore the land north of the Senegal River is arid and in like fashion the Namib and Kalahari Deserts in the south have equally hostile environments. Between the Canary and Benguela currents there is an eastern-flowing countercurrent which brings warmer water to the western coastline from Senegal southward to Zaire and with it very heavy rainfall along this entire coast.

The currents along the Horn of Africa are affected by the

Indian Ocean monsoons. Between November and April cool water flows southwest along the Somali coasts. After April the flow is reversed while the winds continue to be offshore. This produces arid conditions very similar to southwest Africa. The conditions in East Africa south of the equator are completely different. There the temperatures of ocean currents along the coasts of Kenya, Tanzania, and Mozambique are even higher than along the coasts of West Africa. Winds moving over the warm water create onshore warm moist air which provides the rainfall so typical of eastern Africa.

Air pressure zones over the continent are responsible for the winds which acting upon the air masses deny or cause rain. In January there is a high pressure system in the northern hemisphere and a low pressure zone in the southern hemisphere. These pressure systems result in a general airflow over most of the continent from northwest to southeast. In the early months of the year there is hardly any rain in the region between the Atlas Mountains and the equator. At the same time the low pressure zone combined with an onshore air movement creates considerable rainfall in the area south of the equator with the most precipitation in the equatorial lands of Central Africa and the East African highlands. By July the January situation is reversed with a massive low pressure zone over the very hot Sahara. There are two high pressure zones in the southern hemisphere causing an airflow generally from southwest to northeast over Central and West Africa. Rainfall tends to be concentrated in those areas between the equator and the Sahara. Most of the rain falls in the coastal areas from Sierra Leone eastward to the Cameroons where as much as 60 inches during a month is not uncommon. The rainfall slackens as one moves through the western savannah zones and stops completely in the desert. The nearly circular air movement, however, moving over the highlands of Ethiopia causes considerable precipitation.

Although there are wide yearly fluctuations in rainfall over specific areas of the continent, certain valid generalizations can still be made. In that vast area of desert south of the Atlas ranges, in the Kalahari Desert, and in the Horn of Africa there will be on the average less than 10 inches of annual precipitation. The rainy season from the equator north to the desert line is from May to October. South of the equator it is from November through April. In some areas of western and Central Africa there is no definite wet-dry season; the rains are present all year long. There is much seasonal flooding throughout the continent. In only a few places such as along the middle and lower Nile and in the inland delta of the Niger upriver from Timbuktu is it predictable. There is considerable damage done to lands adjacent to most major rivers. Surprisingly there is danger of flooding in areas where the annual rainfall figures would indicate an almost complete absence of precipitation. Short periods of heavy rain in the mountains of the Sahara cause flash flooding in the otherwise dry streambeds which radiate from the highlands. A cascade of flooding water down one of these wadis many miles from the source of rainfall can sweep all before it. Similar flooding has occurred many times over in Ethiopia and throughout East Africa.

More disastrous than floods due to a surplus of rain are the years when the rainfall is below normal. Much of the savannah zone even under the best of circumstances receives only between 10 to 20 inches of annual precipitation. Since this is seasonal the grain and peanut farmers plant their crops to take advantage of the rains and the pastoralists plan to move their herds from place to place based upon access to water. One or two years without adequate water can be borne by the people and animals in an affected zone. However, the drought which began in the mid-1960s lasted in most regions of the Sahel for over seven years. Hundreds of thousands of people died in a broad area stretching from Senegal to Ethiopia. Cattle, sheep, and camel herds, the basis of life for the pastoral people, perished. The drought forced the survivors to abandon their lands and flee to the towns where assistance could be found. This new urban population has become a regular fixture of the savannah towns and cities since most of the people have nothing to return to in their old homelands.

In any casual survey of the factors which limit the African population one cannot ignore temperature and humidity. Most areas of the continent have temperatures throughout the year considerably above the levels necessary to sustain plant growth. Frosts are restricted to the mountains and highlands and violent changes in temperature due to rapid movements of weather fronts such as occur in North America are not present. For most of the continent there is no cold air source. North Africa, due to its proximity, is most affected by the factors which create European weather. The Atlas Mountains, however, block the spread of such storms southward. In the extreme southern part of the continent Mediterranean climate also prevails, and weather there remains moderate even in the winter since the nearest cold-producing area is Antarctica located over 2,000 miles distant.

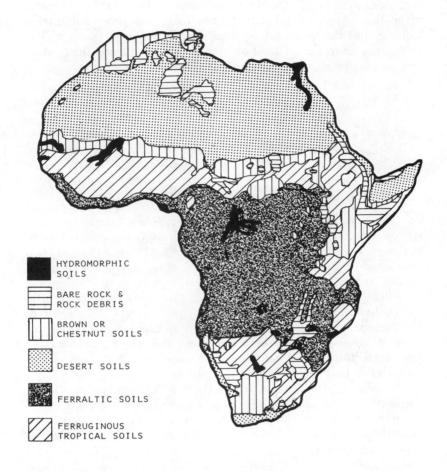

HYDROMORPHIC
SOILS

BARE ROCK &
ROCK DEBRIS

BROWN OR
CHESTNUT SOILS

DESERT SOILS

FERRALTIC SOILS

FERRUGINOUS
TROPICAL SOILS

Simplified Soil Map

With the exception of the highland regions, all the areas south of the Sahara have average surface temperatures in January exceeding 70° F. and these temperatures are increased during and after July. Most of the Sahara remains relatively cool during January but the temperature rises sharply by early summer. The following chart for selected locales gives some idea of the relative average surface temperatures (in Fahrenheit) in Africa:

	January	July
Cairo	55°	82°
In Salah (Sahara)	55	99
Freetown	80	80
Kinshasa	77	81
Salisbury	70	57
Cape Town	72	58
Dar-es-Salaam	82	74

One of the most obvious results of high temperatures in Africa is the rapid evaporation of water from both land and water surfaces. Loss by evaporation from lakes and reservoirs has been estimated at 30 inches per year in the tropics and as much as 80 inches in the Sahara. Ground evaporation is so great that regions receiving between 15 to 20 inches of rain each year are of little agricultural use unless the farmers provide reservoirs for irrigation. In most of tropical Africa the soil is dried out at the beginning of the planting season. Unless the rains are constant afterward, the young plants may die even though the amount of rainfall for that season might be average.

A factor closely related to rainfall is relative humidity. This is a measure of the amount of moisture present in the air at a given moment. The desert areas and the dry savannah have very low humidity. Thus the air seems to burn and wood and other moisture laden materials will warp and crack. Throughout the equatorial forest zones the humidity is high reaching a peak just before the onset of the rainy season. However, the humidity is very high during the day throughout the entire year. The average relative humidity in places such as Lagos, Freetown, Accra, and in the Congo Basin shows normal average humidity of 80 percent or more during all months. A wide variety of fungi grows in extremely humid regions and many materials if left alone will simply rot away. The high temperature—high humidity zones in Africa coincide with the areas of highest population which means that if the nations of equatorial Africa are to prosper, it will be in environments in which most people find it difficult to work. Heat and humidity alone restrict the ability of people to perform well in either sedentary or active occupations.

There are other major problem areas facing modern man in this old continent. Having surveyed, however briefly, the geographic and climatic environment, one can turn to an examination of these with some assurance of understanding their scope and range. For despite the seeming modernity of many of these problems and the concepts held by many African leaders related to the "new African," most are really age-old problems merely raised to higher intensity during the twentieth century. The solutions, if indeed there are solutions to some of Africa's most pressing dilemmas, will be worked out within the parameters of the continent's geography and climatic conditions.

TWO
Population

The African continent is beset with so many problems that perhaps it may be considered fruitless to isolate one as being the most critical, particularly since many are interrelated. However, the more one views critically the non-Western world, the more the question of population demands attention. In all African states the rate of population increase is startling, threatening to neutralize any economic gains made by either the private or government sectors. To those who know little of the dynamics of an African society the solution appears obvious. The birthrate must be lowered to a level approximate with the death rate. Even before progressing to the point of establishing methodologies to this end, any reformer is confronted with a startling, almost insurmountable fact. Most African leaders do not view population increase as a serious threat. Even those who are alarmed find it politically expedient to ignore the problem since any proposals for limiting population are fraught with social, economic, and religious implications which could end the career of an aspiring politician or civil servant.

One fact should be stressed at the outset of any analysis of Africa's population. No one knows the population of the continent with any degree of accuracy. There are a few states such as those in northern Africa, the Republic of South Africa, and Zimbabwe which conduct a regular census and therefore figures from those polities can be taken to be reasonably accurate. Other affluent countries such as Nigeria, Kenya, Senegal, and the Ivory Coast which have a relatively large Western-educated population and who inherited from the colonial regimes sophisticated government machinery have made estimates based upon a variety of constructs which should produce good estimates. For most of the continent, however, the published figures are little more than educated guesses. Those who compile population statistics often accept as their base the last estimates made by the colonial governments before independence was granted. They then apply a simple growth factor and arrive at the population estimate for a specific year. This method ignores the inaccuracy of the original base count. The nature of a pastoral population in the savannah zone mitigates against any accurate count. One major reason why the British or French conducted population surveys was to be able to assess taxes most efficiently. One should not be surprised that many persons evaded colonial census takers. To many Africans the disclosure of any information about one's family to a stranger was to be avoided since this information might be used to harm the family. Another factor which modified the usefulness of the pre-independence estimates was the complex shifting back and forth across arbitrary state boundaries of large numbers of persons. This was particularly the case with the pastoral peoples of the continent's savannah regions.

However useful accurate population figures might be, the collection and publication of a census has many dangers for African governments. This is particularly true when the composition of the legislatures is tied to population statistics. African political leaders surely are aware of the role the census count played in toppling the civilian government of Abubakr Tafewa Balewa of Nigeria in January 1966. The accepted estimate for Nigeria's population in mid-1963 had been slightly more than 37 million people. The census taken during that year indicated to everyone's surprise that Nigeria had a population of over 56 million. The estimate of population in southern Nigeria was reasonably close to the earlier published estimates. However, according to the census the previous estimate in the north had been wrong by a factor of approximately 40 percent and that vast region had a substantially larger population than the south. Reapportionment of seats in the central legislature followed these figures and gave the northern parties total control of the legislature. The 1963 census was, therefore, one major factor leading to the first military coup. A later census in Nigeria was attempted but the results were admittedly so faulty that the figures were never used for any practical purposes. The most credible present estimate of Nigeria's population in 1980 is 75 million persons, but one African demographer believed the country's population to be in excess of 100 million. This vexing question of numbers in Nigeria might be answered by the census projected by its new civilian government.

The example of the questionable accuracy of population figures for Nigeria can be repeated, although with less documentation, for most African states. Any analysis of population in Africa thus must begin with the reality of inaccuracy. However, it is necessary to have some approximate figures in order to discuss rationally the problems of population pressure. Estimates of the continent's total population in 1980 vary from 375 to 450 million persons. If one accepts as reasonable the approximate midpoint between these, one arrives at a figure of 410 million. In 1954 the most accepted estimate of Africa's population had been 224 million. A comparison of these rough figures shows clearly the problem of increase. In a period of a generation the continent's population had almost doubled. The yearly average population increase for Africa in 1979 has been calculated to be between 2.4 and 2.7 percent while many areas such as the Muslim regions of North Africa and the Sudan have even higher rates, some in excess of 3.5 percent annually. If one accepts these statistical constructs as being reasonably accurate, then by the turn of the next century Africa will be the homeland of three-quarters of a billion people.

The present dangerous population inflation began almost a century ago with the "scramble for Africa" by the major European powers. By the opening of the twentieth century all of Africa was arbitrarily divided between France, England, Germany, Portugal, and Belgium. These imperial powers each in its own way immediately after assuming control of the various African territories imposed on them a standarized system of government and laws. Since the boundaries of these new imperial appendages were generally synthetic, each contained a large number of national or tribal groups. Many of these had a long history of antipathy toward one another. They had fought each other and carried off captives either to be used as slaves in their own economies or to be traded to African middlemen or to Europeans for transport to the plantations of the Western Hemisphere. The foundation for European imperial rule through Africa was law and order. European military and police brought an end to the slave trade as well as warfare between tribal groups. An imposed peace settled upon Africa in the twentieth century and this in turn was duly reflected later in an increase in population.

Far more important for the lives of Africans were the advances made in public health. No European power spent any great sums of money to improve the health of Africans. Nevertheless, some distinct advances were made. Governments and missionary groups built hospitals and clinics and sponsored midwife and child care programs in the villages. The discovery of the cause of malaria led to improved mosquito control measures, especially in the towns and cities where European officials lived. Later with the introduction of such suppressives as aralen, paludrin, or chloroquine this greatest of all of Africa's health problems was brought under control. The simple act of drilling wells in the villages or piping water in the cities liberated people from using the polluted water of rivers and streams. The World Health Organization after World War II had a great impact on the health of Africans, particularly in the campaigns against such diseases as smallpox and leprosy. Thus in the half-century before independence the mortality rate particularly among children was greatly reduced. The medical and public health advances, modest though they were, totally upset the previous balance between births and deaths. There was never any concerted attempt during the imperial period to limit the size of families. Any such campaign would have cost too much and would in any case have been against the religious beliefs not only of the Africans, but also of Catholic Europeans. By the early 1920s the problem of overpopulation in some areas was already recognized by colonial officials. Those most aware were normally junior officers in the political, medical, or agricultural branches and therefore they had little to do with formulation of policy. Independence came to most African states in the half-decade after 1957 and the new African political leaders were beset with a host of other problems demanding immediate attention. It was not difficult for them to push the question of population control into the background.

It is almost impossible to project what the continuation of the present rate of growth will mean to an already impoverished African continent. Some idea can be gained by viewing a few specific examples of situations as they exist presently. The first of these relates to the possession of and utilization of land. Most of the clans, tribes, and nations of sub-Saharan Africa have traditionally been sedentary agriculturists. However different their concepts of land-holding, they all tended to look at the land as the source not only of their foodstuff, but also as the giver of life. The earth was generally considered to be divine and land ownership and use was of concern not only to an individual, but to the whole community. African farmers realized how fragile the land was and took steps to protect it from overuse by allowing portions to lie fallow. Until recently the hopes of most young men in African agricultural societies was either to own or be confirmed by the community in a plot of land. For many Africans this is no longer possible.

Alan Paton in one of the most beautiful opening passages in modern literature described the conditions of much of Zululand in *Cry the Beloved Country*. He wrote,

The great red hills stand desolate, and the earth has torn away like flesh. The lightning flashes over them, the clouds pour down upon them, the dead streams come to life, full of the red blood of the earth. Down in the valleys women scratch the soil that is left, and the maize hardly reaches the height of a man.

Such a description could be transferred to many of the homelands of the Republic of South Africa. It is not only that the majority Bantu population of that white-dominated state has only an estimated 13 percent of the arable land of the country that occasions world criticism of the apartheid policy of a succession of South African governments. The African population of South Africa has far outstripped the ability of the available land to support it even had the land remained in the same condition as it was seventy-five years ago.

In less poetic form than Paton's description, agricultural reports from almost all African states tell something of the same story of the systematic rape of the land. There is not just one single reason for denuding much of the land of Kenya, Tanzania, Malawi, Lesotho, Zambia, Sierra Leone, and most other countries of Africa. However, population pressure is one of the major reasons. The desire for land coupled with an exploding population means that land cannot be allowed to lie fallow but must be planted each year. Combined with resistance toward other conservation methods, this led to the step-by-step ruination of already marginal land.

Woodland is fast disappearing, particularly in the savannah areas, as African villagers needing fuel cut down even thorn bushes. Until recently no African state had planned for the reforestation of the savannah. The result is that with the onset of drought conditions much of this land has become semidesert. Even in regions where the land is good the increase in population alone deeply affects the traditional lifestyle of the people. The Kikuyu in Kenya occupy some of the most fertile land in all of Africa and they are skilled farmers. Nevertheless, land is at a premium in the highlands and many young men are forced from the villages because of this scarcity. The reason for this migration is population pressure. Kikuyu population which was estimated at one-half million in 1900 doubled during the first fifty years of this century. The need to regain the lands earlier alienated to white settlers led to the Mau Mau uprising of the 1950s and ultimately to Kenya's independence. By 1972 there were an estimated 2.2 million Kikuyu and the yearly rate of increase is projected at 2.8 percent.

Nigeria provides an even more alarming example of unchecked growth. The estimated census taken by the British in 1921 projected a total population of 18.8 million. This count placed the number of Yoruba at 2.1 million, the Ibo at 3.2 million, and the Hausa at 3.6 million. By 1953 the estimated population was 31.5 million persons. The admittedly flawed 1963 census found almost 56 million people in Nigeria reporting slightly over 6 million for each of the three major nations. If one accepts the present-day low estimate of 75 million persons in Nigeria, then in a period of sixty years there has been an almost fourfold increase in the population.

There are two other immediately noticeable effects of the population explosion. One is the demand by the people that all land not being directly utilized by farmers or herders be converted to their use. Parks or reserves are viewed by most traditional Africans as a waste of good land. Long before independence most of the larger wild animals of West Africa and large sections of Central Africa had already succumbed to the proximity of an ever-growing human population. For the past thirty years the focus of conservationists has been East Africa where the largest herds of animals of most types are to be found. Those who sought to protect some of the endangered species focused upon the poachers who illegally killed the leopard and cheetah for their beautiful skins and the elephant for its ivory. Until recently most have ignored a far more profound threat to the continued existence of wild animals in eastern Africa. The African villager or herdsman wants those lands that are now devoted to wild animals and only the value of tourism has kept land hungry citizens from forcing their governments to restrict the size of the great animal parks or close them entirely. The Masai of southern Kenya, refusing to limit the size of their cattle herds, have already converted large sections of this area into desert where few animals can survive. In the past decade the Masai have also greatly increased the number of their cattle grazing in Tsavo National Park, competing directly with the wild grazers. Some pessimistic Western observers believe that within a generation there will be few wild animals left in eastern Africa, their lands having been appropriated by farmers or herdsmen.

The further reduction or destruction of the wild animal population of Africa, however tragic, does not compare in magnitude with the many problems raised by the second effect of the population explosion. This is the massive migration in all African countries of people from the country districts to the towns and cities. Traditional Africa was rural. The most heavily urbanized of any part of the continent was North Africa where the major cities were over 2,000 years old, having been sustained by the commerce of the Mediterranean world. In the savannah regions south of the Sahara, Muslim traders tried to recreate societies and cultures with which they had been familiar in North Africa or the Persian Gulf. The development of such western Sudanic trading cities of Gao, Timbuktu, Kano, and Katsina was a direct outgrowth of the trans-Saharan trade. In like manner the Zenj cities of Mogadishu, Mombasa, Kilwa, and Sofala in East Africa were created to serve the Indian Ocean trade. In the non-Muslim areas a large congregation of persons in one locale was generally due to the presence of the ruler of one of the great kingdoms. At one time or another the rulers of Dahomey, the Bakongo, the Changamire, or the Zulu demanded the services of a large civil and military bureaucracy at one locale. This phenomenon was unusual when measured by the usual patterns of African life. The Yoruba of western Nigeria seem an exception to the general rule concerning African urbanization. They had already shown in the early nineteenth century a preference for urban living as their development of the towns of Oyo, Ibadan, Abeokuta, Iwo, and Lagos attest.

Most of the great cities of sub-Saharan Africa are modern creations of European imperialism. Many such as Ft. Lamy, Kaduna, Enugu, Entebbe, Bujumbura, and Lusaka became important because they were the seats of government. Others such as Dakar, Freetown, Lagos, Port Harcourt, and Luanda were valuable ports in addition to being the center of government activity in a given locale. Some like Nairobi and Port Harcourt did not even exist before the imperial power decided to establish a city. Port Harcourt in eastern Nigeria grew because the British needed a port in that region and Nairobi because it was an important highland campsite during the building of the railway from Mombasa to Uganda.

From the beginnings of European rule the cities drew population from the countryside. The administrative establishments needed Africans to staff the low level positions in government. European companies also needed clerks and laborers since most only maintained skeleton staffs of European managers. Although in parts of Africa a money economy had been operative for centuries along the coastline, it had not penetrated inland to any degree before the twentieth century. During the imperial period barter systems became secondary. Most goods, particularly European luxury items, had a definite money value attached. If Africans wanted to possess any of those desirable products they had to obtain money. Another incentive for the acquisition of money was the taxing systems of the European overloads. Each imperial power very early in its tenure decided to make the Africans share in the expense of government and demanded the payment of taxes in money. Where there had been developed export crops such as cocoa, tea, rubber, peanuts, or coffee, money could be obtained by growing these or working on rural farms or plantations. Even in agriculturally rich areas as Ghana, western Nigeria, the Ivory Coast, Rhodesia, or Kenya, one of the easiest ways of obtaining money was to move either temporarily or permanently into one of the cities and become a hired worker.

Increasing educational opportunities available to Africans particularly in British and French territories also contributed to the exodus from the rural areas to the cities. During the twentieth century the size of the government establishments in each African territory also grew considerably as did the private economic sectors. Thus for many young men the lure of the cities was not a figment of their imaginations. For some of them there did exist considerable opportunity. However, for most, the opportunities were never as great as believed. Even before the great depression of the 1930s there was a considerable redundant urban population which could not be employed and which managed to survive largely because of the general African commitment to family sharing. If one member of a family were working, no matter how distant was the connection, he had a responsibility toward all of his relatives who were not so fortunate.

The trend toward overpopulation of the cities begun during the imperial period increased in the years after independence. In most states the size of the government bureaucracy grew in the period following 1960. Localized prosperity in some regions caused the influx of migrants to increase dramatically in a very short period. The copper industry of Zaire and Zambia, petroleum in Nigeria, and tourism in Kenya created hundreds of thousands of jobs at all levels which had to be filled. Major centers of business or ports such as Cairo, Salisbury, Lagos, Dakar, or Abidjan reflected the increasing propserity of the past two decades and offered skilled and unskilled Africans opportunities far beyond those available in the towns or country villages. At the same time disasters both natural and man-made contributed to overcrowding of some cities by the victims. The most dramatic natural catastrophe was the Sahel drought in the decade after 1965. In many areas the nomadic way of life perished forever and the refugees flooded into the smaller inadequately prepared towns and cities where they form a depressed class with few skills in regions which never offered opportunities for many jobs. From Senegal to Ethiopia the survivors of the drought form an alien group in newly constructed slum areas in all the major border towns. Africa's many wars and political disturbances have left behind hundreds of thousands of refugees. Persons with no land, with few skills, and little hope are the legacy of the conflicts in Ethiopia, Zaire, Chad, Somalia, and Uganda. Even affluent Nigeria has had considerable trouble dealing with the movement of population in the wake of its bloody, protracted civil war.

The overpopulation of the cities of Africa is one of the most noticeable phenomena of the past generation. No city in Africa has escaped, but some have been affected more than others. Lagos, the capital city of Nigeria, in 1953 had an estimated population of one-quarter million persons. Ninety miles north, Ibadan, the most populous city in black Africa, was slightly larger. By 1972 the population of Lagos had grown to 1.2 million and Ibadan contained more than 800,000 persons. To those familiar with West Africa, these cities became synonymous with the worst in overcrowding, poor transportation, and a host of other evils associated with poor urban planning, far outstripping the conditions to be found in Dakar, Accra, Freetown, Abidjan, and Douala. Nairobi, the fabled city of modern Kenya, grew from 135,000 people in 1953 to over one-half million twenty years later. In the same period Algiers increased from 350,000 to 1.9 million, Cairo from 2.5 million to 5 million, Salisbury from 160,000 to more than one-half million, and greater Johannesburg from 900,000 to 1.4 million.

The results of rapid population growth are obvious. No African government, even had it committed huge sums and had large, well-organized functioning planning and building depart-

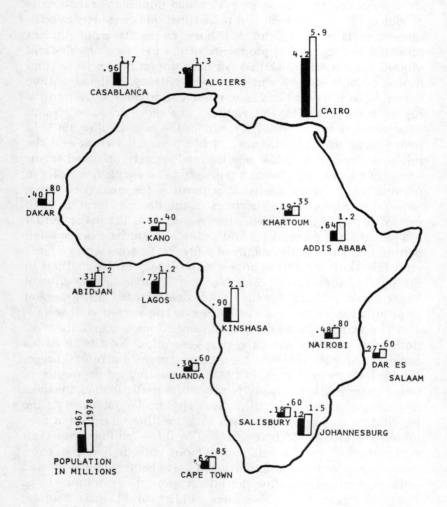

CASABLANCA .96 1.7

ALGIERS .96 1.3

CAIRO 4.2 5.9

DAKAR .40 .80

KHARTOUM .19 .35

KANO .30 .40

ADDIS ABABA .64 1.2

ABIDJAN .31 1.2

LAGOS .75 1.2

KINSHASA .90 2.1

NAIROBI .48 .80

DAR ES SALAAM .27 .60

LUANDA .30 .60

SALISBURY .18 .60

JOHANNESBURG 1.2 1.5

1967 1978
POPULATION
IN MILLIONS

CAPE TOWN .62 .85

Urban Population

ments, could have kept up with the population increase. In all of Africa's major cities basic housing, water supplies, and sanitary facilities lagged far behind the needs of the people. The problems of providing rudimentary health services, public transportation, and fire and police protection for these new, thrown together suburbs were usually beyond the skills and capacity of any African government. Far from being areas of golden opportunities, the cities have become within a few years of independence veritable sinkholes for the aspirations of generations of Africans.

The surface problems of most African cities are all too obvious. The road and street systems were inadequate even for the numbers of automobiles present fifteen years ago. With the great increase in the numbers of vehicles and the African's dependence upon them has come unimagined traffic problems. Short trips of a few miles can take hours in Lagos, Kinshasa, or Ibadan. The larger portion of most cities are slums when measured by Western standards. The streets are unpaved, houses crowded together, water supplies inadequate, and sewage disposal rudimentary. The crime rate as calculated by reference to either petty or major violations has increased many times over. There are not enough police to curb the growing lawlessness and such Draconian measures as public executions have failed to halt even the relatively minor crimes of thievery and burglary. In South Africa many of the African sections adjacent to the major cities are considered to be too dangerous after dark for regular police patrols.

The hidden effects of the overcrowding of the cities are perhaps even more dangerous than those which are apparent. Although the exact unemployment figures for any major city are unknown, they are obviously quite high. Some experts have claimed that over 40 percent of young men in the larger coastal towns of West Africa are unemployed. It is beyond the capacity of most African states to increase substantially the number of jobs available in the public or private sectors. Therefore almost all of those who are presently unemployed will remain without work. Inflation in most African cities is another factor which plagues both those with and without jobs. Since the first impact of the price rise occasioned by the OPEC increases of the early 1970s, the annual inflation rate has soared in all African states. In Ghana in 1979 it was estimated at over 200 percent while Uganda's rate had reached the astronomical level of 700 percent. Surrounded by evidences of material well-being and denied means of obtaining highly desired goods, the unemployed and occasionally employed can easily become radicalized. Increasingly frustrated, they can make demands on all levels of government far beyond the capacity of its agencies. If quick solutions are not obtained then they are a potential danger to any government, particularly one like Kofi Busia's in Ghana some years ago whose policies appeared to counter the demands of the masses.

If the foregoing generalized account is reasonably accurate then what does this mean for the future of most African countries? The trends are there for all to see. Population will continue to increase alarmingly. Perhaps it could be checked if Africa's rulers would admit that population growth is a problem, but it is difficult for the military or civilian leaders of Africa to become overly concerned with what may happen in ten or twenty years. They are confronted with what appear to be more pressing matters, not the least of which is trying to stay in power. The leaders of Africa for a variety of political, educational, religious, and historical reasons do not bring unfettered enthusiasm to the question of population control. It is, therefore, not surprising to discover that little is being done to educate the population of any state or to provide easy access to and instruction about birth control methods for persons who might wish to limit the size of their families. Even if there were extant in any African country a massive government supported program there would still be great difficulty in effecting any substantial population limitation. India affords the best example of the general failure to convince people to abandon age-old beliefs and practices. Despite well-articulated educational programs and the expenditure of tremendous sums over the past thirty years there has been only limited success. India's example can be projected directly to Africa since both huge areas share certain common features. The many different societies of each are dependent upon poor land, utilize relatively primitive methods of agriculture, have a high illiteracy rate, and have concepts of masculinity reinforced by social, religious, and economic factors which demand large families.

Although it is not prudent for any observer to attempt specific predictions about the future of any part of Africa, the trends in population growth do point to certain observations and conclusions. It appears obvious that no African government in the near future will make serious attempts to control the increasing number of children being born, to direct the settlement of and better use of marginal land, or to halt the influx of people into the cities. A state which on a per capita basis is poor today will grow poorer, the land will become less fertile, and more people will flood into the cities. This will mean that even the more affluent states must maintain a growth in their Gross National Product of over 3 percent annually just to remain even. It is difficult to believe that the increasing numbers of poor, disappointed persons will continue to remain quiescent. It is more probable that they will become even poorer and more despairing and willing to follow political leaders of dubious merit who promise a surcease to their suffering. The increasing poor of Africa will probably become an even more important contributing factor to the political instability of African states. It is very easy for African experts to concentrate their attention upon more immediate challenges and be sanguine about the dangers of the continued growth of population and to indulge in the optimistic rhetoric so typical of many of the world's leaders. The reality is that few persons even see the escalating populations as threatening, postponing any substantive remedial action. The starvation and disorder attendant upon the Sahel drought could be a portent not just for a portion of the continent, but for all of Africa.

THREE
Ethnic and Cultural Diversity

There has been a systematic development of new myths to replace the older stereotypes in the nearly two decades since most African states gained their independence. One of the most prevalent concerns the nature of the African population. Despite overwhelming evidence available to even the most casual traveler there is the persistent belief in the existence of one dominant ethnic group for the entire continent. Further conventional wisdom creates an idyllic past where Africans lived in peace and harmony with one another until the arrival of white imperialists who for their own selfish interests created arbitrary divisions among the African populations. Not discounting the modicum of truth in the claims that Europeans used the native people to gain specific goals which were not always in the best interests of the Africans, one can say that the myth of unity is one of the most difficult of Africa's problems. Millions of non-African people, particularly descendents of African slaves in the Western Hemisphere, searching for their past, want to believe in African homogeneity. African leaders since the 1950s have for political reasons emphasized Pan-Africanism and downplayed nationalism and diversity. However convenient it is to hold on to such beliefs, it is necessary to discard most of them if one is to understand the rich diversity of the African past, many of Africa's current problems, and realistic hopes for future development.

The best present evidence points to Africa as the continent of man's genesis. Although there are no direct interconnections between the man-apes who lived in eastern Africa over two and one-half million years ago and modern man, it appears that representatives of the five major ethnic types are identifiable as early as 10,000 B.C. By then Caucasian agriculturists and town dwellers in North Africa had migrated westward from older Middle Eastern settlements. However, by far the most widespread of any population group were the Capoid or Bushmanoid hunters and gatherers who ranged in small bands throughout most of the continent. Some experts speculate that the Bushmanoid was the base population of Africa and that the modern-day Negro, Khoisan, and Pygmy populations developed from it. Isolation of certain Bushmanoid groups from their neighbors over long periods of time allowed for the development of people radically different from the parent population. The ancestors of the many differing types of Negro people were present in western Africa's savannah regions by the tenth century B.C. Some of these early Negroes were the first people in sub-Saharan Africa either to develop on their own or to borrow from North Africa the skills of agriculture and domestication of animals. Thus provided with a more secure food supply, the Negro population grew rapidly. They were taller and heavier than their Bushmanoid neighbors. The future of most of sub-Saharan Africa thus belonged to the agrarian Negro.

The Bushmanoid population in all parts of the continent in the ensuing centuries altered their ways very little and could not cope with the technically superior and more powerful competitive Negro groups. During the past 2,000 years the various Negro clans and tribes in a bewildering series of migrations filled up most of the African continent. The Bushmanoid groups were either destroyed, assimilated, or driven into areas not coveted by the Negro. A remnant of the Bushmanoid was the parent population for the present day Hottentot (Khoi) and Bushman (San) of the desert regions of southern Africa. In their long journey to escape the Negro, some of the Hottentots acquired the skills of cattle keeping. By the time of the first European visits of the sixteenth century The Hottentots occupied most of the area which later became Cape Colony. Subsequent colonization by the Dutch and English eventually robbed the Hottentots of their lands and cattle. In the nineteenth century the Hottentots intermarried with whites, Negroes, and Asians and thus became the mixed Cape Colored population of today. The Bushmen never acquired skills other than hunting and gathering. They were considered nuisances by the Hottentots, Negroes, and later Europeans. Each group hunted them mercilessly. Their remnants are found today in small scattered bands roaming the Kalahari Desert and the regions of the Okavango swamp. Intermarriage with the Negro populations of Namibia has in the twentieth century further reduced the numbers of wandering Bushmen and it is conceivable that within a generation these tiny gatherers and their way of life will have totally disappeared.

In all probability another offshoot of the Bushmanoid population was the Pygmy. As with all hunters and gatherers, the basic Pygmy societal and governmental unit was the extended family. Some of these groups many centuries ago became isolated from one another. Intermarriage within some of these small groups over hundreds of years preserved certain characteristics such as delicate bone structure and small stature. Like their Bushmanoid neighbors, the Pygmies were forced into the most inhospitable areas by the many migrations of the more numerous and powerful Negro subgroups. They retreated deep into the forests of Central Africa and adapted their societies to this hostile environment long before the Bantu moved into the forests in any great numbers. Today the Pygmies are to be found in the Ituri Forest of Zaire and in neighboring Rwanda and Burundi. They are also fast disappearing because of intermarriage with their dominant Negro neighbors.

Sub-Saharan Africa has been dominated by the Negro population for thousands of years. They had learned agriculture and animal domestication and these twin skills enabled them, in time, to dominate their less knowledgeable neighbors. Early agriculture was almost exclusively devoted to planting and harvesting various types of grain which could survive the conditions of the savannah. Thus when population pressure grew too great in one region, some of the excess would simply move to other savannah locales. Some Negro groups came to specialize in pastoralism and many adopted the habit of keeping cattle, sheep, and goats, while not giving up their main source of livelihood, the planting of crops. This Neolithic Revolution was responsible in Africa as it had been elsewhere in the world for fundamental changes in the lifestyles of Africans. They had to settle down in one locale for a part of the year in order to harvest their crops. In time the security given by a guaranteed food supply caused a rapid increase in the population. Sophisticated religions were devised, land became valuable, and more complex systems of government evolved. Iron was introduced to the Negro communities of West Africa some time just before the beginnings of the Christian era. This increased the agriculturist's command over his environment even further. The need for more land was accentuated and different Negro groups began to replicate themselves in new colonies.

There were many other reasons why Negro villagers moved from one place to another. Political and religious differences and wars also contributed, but the major factor in most migrations remained the need for or desire for land. In western and central Africa for more than a thousand years the migrations generally occurred only in the savannah lands. Although there were some adventuresome people who moved into the forest fringes, the settlement of the forest areas of Africa had to wait for the introduction of East Indian foodstuffs such as bananas, plantains, and yams. The movement into the forest zones began sometime after the fourth century A.D. in East Africa and continued well into the nineteenth century in parts of West and Central Africa. Two vital points must be made about all the migrations. The first is that populating of the bulk of the continent took many centuries. The second is that there were many different migrations. Differences between various Negro groups had already developed in the original homelands. Thus migrations overlapped one another and obviously caused many different wars as hostile bands struggled for the same land.

In western Africa the ancestors of the present day Mande, Gur, Akan, Yoruba, Ibo, and other Negro groups moved slowly from the interior savannah lands toward the coasts. Some of these had already arrived in their present locations before 1000 A.D. The Yoruba, for example, created the large viable kingdom of Ife soon after this date. The state was sophisticated enough by the twelfth century to produce some of the world's finest examples of naturalistic art. Contrarywise, some West African people like groups of Mande and the Fante were still moving into the coastal savannah zones when the Europeans first arrived in the fifteenth century. All these western African people differed vastly from one another in their specific religious and political beliefs, and each major group spoke differing languages. The basic societal unit for most of these, however, remained the agricultural village. Some had transcended this type of organization and had evolved major kingdoms long before the first Portuguese explorer ventured south of Cape Blanco. Ghana, Mali, Songhai, the Hausa states, and Ife all had had a complex functioning bureaucracy whose leader was a divinely chosen king who ruled over vast territories inhabited by hundreds of thousands of people.

During the period when these various Negro groups were slowly but inexorably filling up the vacant lands of West Africa and evolving their particularistic complex societal and political systems, an even more dramatic set of migrations was taking place. These were the movement of Bantu-speaking subgroups from their homeland near Lake Chad into central, eastern, and

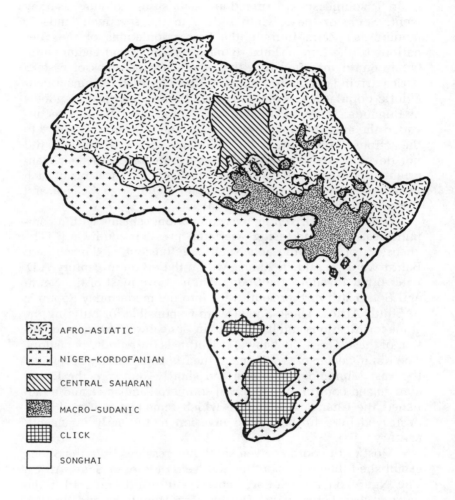

AFRO–ASIATIC

NIGER–KORDOFANIAN

CENTRAL SAHARAN

MACRO–SUDANIC

CLICK

SONGHAI

Language Families According to Greenberg

eventually southern Africa. In a series of extremely complex migrations lasting over 1,500 years, Bantu groups moved generally in a southeastward direction establishing colonies as they went. Some of these Bantu settled in the savannah lands of modern-day Zaire forming the base populations of the later nations of the Lunda, Luba, Bemba, Kazembe, and Ovimbundu. Other Bantu migrated into the interlacustrine areas of eastern Africa driving out or absorbing the already settled Bushmanoid or Nilotic populations. Eventually they formed the great kingdoms of Buganda, Bunyoro, Ankole, and Toro. Other Bantu later invaded the areas of modern-day Kenya and Tanzania. Contrary to the actions of the Bantu of the great lakes region, these Bantu did not develop great kingdoms but were satisfied with their clan-oriented political systems. These clans were the ancestors of such present-day peoples as the Kikuyu, Luo, Hehe, Gogo, Chagga, and many even more fragmented polities.

Other clans, driven by overpopulation, schisms within communities, and increasing warfare, pressed southward. The ancestors of the Sotho and Nguni subdivisions of the southern Bantu were present in Zimbabwe by the eleventh century A.D. Later other invaders, the Shona Bantu, drove most of the Nguni and Sotho still further southward into the modern-day Republic of South Africa. These Shona were responsible for building the stone fortifications and living sites in Zimbabwe. The most important of these, Great Zimbabwe, still attracts the wonder of visitors. The Karanga clan of the Shona in the fifteenth century developed the vast Monomotapa empire and shortly afterward the Rozwi clan seized control over much of southern Zimbabwe and established the Changamire empire which remained powerful until destroyed by a further Bantu invasion in the early nineteenth century.

Most of the Sotho driven south by pressures from the Shona established themselves on the high veld of interior South Africa. The Nguni on the contrary moved southward and settled the narrow strip between the Drakensberg Mountains and the sea. Both Sotho and Nguni were agriculturists but individual clans of each became skilled cattle herders. The basic social and political organization of each was the clan, some of which in the eighteenth century had become very large, outgrowing mere kinship ties. In the latter part of that century Nguni Xosa clans made their first real contacts with the eastward-moving white Afrikaner farmers. The ensuing Bantu-white conflicts in South Africa lasted for almost a century. The most prolonged and dramatic of these were the nine Kaffir wars along the eastern frontier of Cape Colony. These wars marked clearly the end of relatively free unoccupied land for the Bantu.

While population pressure still continued, the open frontier disappeared in the nineteeth century. Even before encountering Afrikaner colonists, the expansion of one Bantu clan was always done at the expense of those who already occupied the land. The seventeenth and eighteenth centuries saw the escalation of larger, more costly wars throughout sub-Saharan Africa. These clashes not only rewarded the victors with land but in many areas, particularly in West and Central Africa, provided captives who could be sold to African, Arab, or European slavers. Successful Negro clans expanded into new territories, conquered the inhabitants, and incorporated many of the defeated clans into new states. Thus some clans grew very large and could more properly be referred to as tribes or nations. In West Africa the wars and the slave trade aided the development of the powerful states of Ashanti, Dahomey, Oyo, and Benin. In Central Africa the various Luba, Lunda, and Kimbundu kingdoms also participated actively in the Atlantic slave trade. The Kazembe, Bemba, Lozi, and Yao states had their genesis late in the eighteenth century due to the generally unsettled conditions of life in Central Africa.

The most dramatic changes of all occurred in southern Africa where war chiefs seized power and formed nations by conquest. The greatest of these rulers was Shaka who by his military conquests created the Zulu nation in slightly over a decade. Other Sotho and Nguni chiefs soon adopted the methodologies of the Zulu and there ensued a series of catastrophic wars generally called the *Mfecane* or time of crushing. Hundreds of thousands of Bantu died in the 1820s and 1830s. Vast tracts of land were depopulated and left open for the Afrikaner trekkers to seize. When the *Mfecane* ended there were left in its wake such Bantu nations as the Basuto, Zulu, Swazi, Pondo, and Xosa. Some new nations were created far from the source of the *Mfecane* by groups fleeing the carnage. The Shangaan state developed in Mozambique, and another reverse Nguni migration destroyed the Changamire empire before the invaders settled near Lake Malawi. A further group, the Makalolo, cut their way through the Lozi clans before coming to rest in the upper Zambesi area. The last of the offshoots of the *Mfecane* was that of the Ndebele who in the wake of the destruction of the Changamire established a powerful nation modeled upon Zulu concepts in southern Zimbabwe.

Caucasian settlements of the continent, although not as complex as that of the Negro, nevertheless have a long history. The first Caucasians moved across the Sinai peninsula from the Middle East perhaps as early as 10,000 B.C. They built towns, organized agriculture, and engaged in both the seaborne and interior trades. The great Egyptian civilization was created by one group of these semitic invaders while elsewhere smaller kingdoms grew into some prominence. Carthaginians, Romans, Greeks, and Vandals all established hegemony over parts of northern Africa and each had its genetic and cultural contributions to make to the most numerous population group which has been given the name Berber. Then in the seventh century there began the most important of all the semitic invasions. The followers of Muhammad conquered the entirety of North Africa and despite radical political shifts, their religion and culture has dominated the southern Mediterranean for over thirteen centuries. North African merchants were soon busy trading for ivory, gold, and slaves across the Sahara. Slowly over the next seven centuries after the conquest, these Arab merchants spread their economic control, intermarried with the sudanic black population, and brought Islam to the very edge of the forest zones.

Ethiopia is another area of Caucasian settlement. Even before the Christian era semitic colonizers from Yemen had established themselves along the coastline of the Red Sea. Over many centuries this base population adopted Christianity and created a complex centralized state before being driven into the highlands by Islamic invasions of the eighth century. Through many vicissitudes the Ethiopians evolved a unique Christian kingdom in the fortress of the mountains, one which endured until the third quarter of the twentieth century. During the late nineteenth century "scramble for Africa" the Ethiopians not only maintained their independence but were competitors with European powers expanding their control over non-Ethiopian areas until the present-day boundaries of the state were reached.

A third area of Caucasian influence was the East African coastline where beginning as early as the eighth century A.D. merchants from the Persian Gulf established trading stations. Eventually some of these became major cities where hundreds of Muslim settlers mediated between the interior and Indian Ocean trade. Such cities as Mogadishu, Mombasa, Kilwa, Zanzibar, and Sofala came to attract thousands of Bantu who supplied the work force in these prospering towns. In time there evolved along the East African coast a hybrid population, culture, and language called Swahili. Each of these trading cities maintained its political independence until the southernmost were occupied by the Portuguese in the sixteenth century. The central and northern city-states after a century of warfare with the Portuguese retained their political uniqueness until brought under the centralizing control of the Sultan of Zanzibar in the early nineteenth century. However different they were from one another, these city-states shared certain common features. The black population was dominated by a small "Arab" oligarchy. The ruler of each separate state and later the Sultan of Zanzibar was not concerned with territory but with trade; thus the interior Bantu states such as the Kikuyu, Hehe, Gogo, and Chagga were left relatively undisturbed until the slave trade became an important factor in East Africa. Even then the Sultan and his business associates were most interested in trade, not conquest. In the nineteenth century East African merchants opened trade stations throughout East and Central Africa, some as far distant as central Zaire. Everywhere the merchants went they took with them the Swahili language and the Muslim religion.

The most recent of European contacts with Africa are those begun by the Portuguese explorers of the fifteenth century. With only one major exception, European interest in Africa during the next four centuries was concerned with trade. Very soon after the opening of West Africa to European mariners and traders, the trade in slaves became dominant. Europeans soon learned that raiding for captives was counter-productive. African traders would supply them with all the slaves desired. Once the complex arrangements had been made for the trade in Senegambia, the Gold Coast, Dahomey, Nigeria, or Angola, African rulers and businessmen discouraged explorations of the interior, fearing that the European merchants would bypass their African counterparts. This is the major reason why Africa remained the "Dark Continent" throughout that period in time when millions of Africans were being purchased along its coasts and removed to the New World. Most of the coastal areas where the trade was conducted were hot, humid, and unhealthy which is a further reason why no European power during the mercantilistic period ever seriously pursued colonization plans.

The term colonialism has come to be used erroneously to describe the period of European hegemony over Africa. In fact, even in the twentieth century there were only a few African areas which could accurately be described as colonies. The French were very successful in transplanting millions of colons to Algeria during their 125 years of control. The Portuguese government tried very hard in the period of the Salazar regime to colonize Mozambique and Angola, but had very questionable success. Colonization efforts in Kenya and Zimbabwe also belong to the twentieth century. Even in these very healthy highland areas the number of whites was not large enough for them to sustain their domination of the government during the period when Britain was shedding its control of its dependent empire. Mau Mau violence in Kenya and a decade of guerrilla warfare in Zimbabwe removed the minority Caucasian population from their favored positions. There was only one area of sub-Saharan Africa where colonialism could be considered a success. This was the territory which is now the Republic of South Africa.

Colonialism worked in South Africa for a variety of reasons. In the first place the climate is good, the land productive, and most of the region is healthy. The Dutch at first did not want to colonize, they simply brought in settlers in order to aid in supplying the East Indian bound ships with food. Before state-aided emigration was halted in the early eighteenth century there was a substantial body of white settlers. Good land and climate and a favorable trading location caused the small white nucleus to grow enormously in that century, thus forcing the Hottentots off the land in the Cape region. The British assumed responsibility for the government of the Cape as a result of the Napoleonic Wars with far-reaching results. The more liberal British attitudes resulted in the abolition of slavery and more lenient treatment of the dispossessed Hottentots. The century after the final British takeover in 1814 witnessed the Hottentots moving to the towns and cities, merging with other ethnic groups to form the Cape Colored population. Even more dramatic events directly related to British rule culminated in the Great Trek. Many of the predominantly Dutch farmers (Boers) were dissatisfied with the changes made in the government and the law. They resented English becoming the official language. The liberal attitudes toward Hottentots and the abolition of slavery were enough to convince thousands to pack their belongings and move deep into the interior of the continent. These Boer Trekkers in the 1830s defeated the powerful Zulu and Ndebele nations and created their own republics. Much of the history of southern Africa from that time forward concerns the antipathy of the British and the Boers. The British desire to control the activities of the Boers increased after the discovery of diamonds and gold in the republics. British-Boer rivalry culminated in the Boer War (1898–1902) which ended the independence of the republics but left a legacy of bitterness among the Boer people.

After 1870 there was a rapid development of the economy, first of the Cape and then, with the discovery of gold, of the northermost territory, the Transvaal. This was accompanied in the twentieth century by a very great increase in the white population. Mining, particularly for gold, underwrote the industrial development of South Africa to the point where that country is today the industrial giant of Africa. The present economic dominance of South Africa is due not only to the blessings of a full range of minerals, European expertise, and capital, but also to the readily available black work force. The movement to the cities so noticeable in the past twenty years in the areas north of the Limpopo River began much earlier in South Africa. All of the major industrial and commercial firms depend upon Bantu workers who have crowded into the areas immediately adjacent to all the towns and cities of the republic.

The Act of Union of 1910 created a unitary state called the Union of South Africa from the four previously separate colonies. An ironic twist of fate gave the Afrikaner-speaking population (Boers) control of the central government. They have never relinquished this and thus the victors of the Boer War found themselves by the end of World War I in a minority position in South Africa. The election of 1948 turned out a moderate coalition central government and gave power to the Nationalist Party which represented a narrow Afrikaner bias. The party was also pledged to institute a policy of separation (apartheid) between white and black. The decade after the election witnessed the establishment of that system designed to exclude the Cape Colored and Bantu permanently from claiming a large share in the economic future of the country and taking away many of the rights formerly enjoyed by the Bantu and Hottentots. Independence from Britain was secured and a Republic was declared in 1961.

The scramble for Africa in the 1890s resulted in the arbitrary parceling out of lands to various European states. Boundaries were drawn with no consideration given to the African people. Thus a boundary line could cut a national or tribal unit into two parts. In an extreme case, the Ewe people of western Africa were placed under three differing European administrations. The

European powers in the non-colonial areas of Africa were content in the twentieth century to try to extract enough funds from their charges to pay for administration. All tried to come to some agreements with the traditional rulers and created types of rule which combined traditional and modern elements of governments. Each state introduced its own legal and political system and required all the Africans to abide by some general rules of behavior. Compliance with the orders of the government was forced by a central police force and in some cases by army units. Thus the facade of unity was created in all these dependent areas. However, the European powers were never able to establish a genuine spirit of harmony among many of the African groups who lived within the confines of the arbitrary boundaries. This was particularly true of some of the larger dependencies such as the Belgian Congo, Nigeria, and the Sudan, or in territories such as Rwanda, Burundi, or Uganda where the competitive social systems dictated continuing hostility. Intertribal warfare was ended only because the Africans were afraid of the retribution of the European police.

One unintended outcome of the European occupation of Africa was the division of the continent into specific linguistic zones. The French, British, Belgian, and Portuguese dependencies had to be governed and obviously each of these European states transferred their governmental, legal, and economic concepts to the new territories, but most importantly, these areas were governed within the context of a specific language. The boundaries which divided a single African tribe or nation into subdivisions also dictated that the preferred language for each group would be that of the European conqueror. Thus by the time of independence the educated African on either side of an arbitrary boundary had been separated from his kinsmen by the acceptance of two differing dominant European languages.

During most of their short tenure of slightly more than one-half a century, none of the European powers gave much thought to training Africans to assume the responsibility of governing themselves. On the contrary, until after World War II, they supported the traditional rulers of the many divergent tribal groups. None of the imperial powers followed a consistent pattern of giving Western educations to large numbers of Africans or even training in anything but the lowest level jobs. Thus when France, Britain, and Belgium with inordinate haste granted independence to their former territories in the decade after 1955, they left behind a vacuum of power. The old animosities reappeared and the new independent governments of Africa found that these made a mockery of nationalistic and Pan-African claims.

Much space has been devoted to this very general recounting of the history of African peoples because without such a guide it is not possible to understand the problems of human, cultural, and religious diversity which have so plagued the continent in the past two decades. However different the various independent governments of Africa are, they share one common problem. This is how to create a sense of loyalty to the new states which will transcend local or tribal loyalties. Very soon after independence most African political leaders gave up all but token observance of the concept of Pan-Africanism and instead concentrated upon the task of creating unity out of diversity within their own states. In no African state has the government, either civilian or military, been entirely successful in doing this. In some the tribal or national diversity has been so great that the central authorities have not been able to prevent civil wars or genocide. Almost immediately after independence the present state of Zaire was wracked by civil wars which lasted almost five years, the solution of which threatened even the continued existence of the United Nations. The Biafran War was a civil war which pitted the Ibo, Ibibio, Ijaw and other eastern peoples against their countrymen from the western and northern regions of Nigeria. That war resulted in the destruction of hundreds of thousands of people and the expenditures of millions of dollars before the Biafrans were forced back into the Nigerian federation. There were some examples of genocide from the conflict in Zaire, but the two areas which best epitomize this evil would be the small former Belgian possessions of Rwanda and Burundi. In each of these the Watutsi and Bahutu peoples carried out pogroms designed to exterminate one another with the resultant wanton killing of hundreds of thousands and forced evacuation of even more to neighboring states.

The arbitrary boundaries drawn by the imperial powers during the "scramble" have been a constant source of friction between states since they violated tribal and historic realities. Algeria and Morocco engaged in minor skirmishing over Saharan territory and Uganda and Tanzania had a number of relatively small-scale border flare-ups before the Tanzanian invasion of 1979 overthrew the despotic regime of Idi Amin. Perhaps the most long-lasting and dangerous boundary disputes have focused upon Ethiopia. In the mid-1890s Ethiopia successfully defended itself against Italian expansionism despite the fact that the coastal region of Eritrea was retained by Italy. Soon after the Italian defeat at Adowa, the Emperor Menelik sent his armies into non-Ethiopian lands and thus laid claim by conquest to territory outside the highlands that had never belonged to Ethiopia and which was populated by non-Ethiopian peoples. Chief among these conquered people were the Somalis who had to endure the occupation of their arid lands by the British, French, Italians, and Ethiopians. The British and Italian areas were merged in 1960 to form the Somali Republic and soon afterward the Somali government began to agitate for a return of their lands. This caused some friction with Kenya over Somalia's southern boundary but the most difficulty was with Ethiopia over its Haud and Ogaden Provinces conquered by Menelik, sparsely inhabited with the largest population group being the Somalis. Revolutions in Ethiopia and the intrusion of the cold war into the region played important roles in triggering the disastrous war between Somalia and Ethiopia in 1978. However, the major reason was Somali irredentism—the desire to regain territory and people lost almost one hundred years ago. The same reasons caused the Eritrean revolution against the imposition of Ethiopian control in 1971. The Somali War fought with heavy casualties on both sides resulted in a flood of displaced persons pouring into Somalia, creating the largest single refugee problem in Africa in the 1980s. The war, however, ended after eight months of fighting and while the issues are still unresolved, a further conflict is unlikely in the near future. This is not the case in Eritrea where the decade-old civil war continues to bleed an already impoverished Ethiopia and shows little sign of being brought to a conclusion in the near future.

Another arena where boundary arrangements made by a European power and sanctioned by some African states has led to open warfare is in the Western Sahara. Formerly called the Spanish Sahara, this desert land has a small population and phosphate is its only resource. The Spanish government under pressure from African states decided in 1976 to withdraw and negotiated a boundary settlement with Morocco and Mauritania whereby each of these states would assume control of a portion of its former colonial appendage. They did not take into account the goals of an organization claiming to represent the local people. Supported by Algeria, the guerrilla forces of the Polisario have regained a large portion of the territory, caused the near breakdown of government in Mauritania, and at present force the

Moroccan government to station a large portion of its army in the Western Sahara.

The historic advance of Islam across the Sahara has created major divisive problems in a wide belt of territory from West Africa to the Horn of Africa. Islam can be a unifying factor cutting across state and tribal boundaries, but it can also serve to widen the gulf already existing between differing peoples. Every state in the northern Sudanic zone is plagued by a generalized division of its people according to both ethnic and religious standards. The population of the northern areas in all such states is predominantly Berber or Arab in origin and Muslim. The southern regions are inhabited by a large number of differing Negro groups who are mainly animists with some Christians in leadership roles. When independence was granted to most of these states, the more populous southern regions where the bulk of the Western-educated lived came to control the governments. Tensions between north and south have been an important factor in the governments of Mali, Dahomey, Ghana, Niger, and Nigeria. Wherever the Islamic northerners were in the majority as in Nigeria, they wrested power from the southerners. When the power relations were almost equally divided such as in Dahomey, the central government became weak, almost powerless to act effectively.

In two areas, the Sudan and Chad, the differences between northerners and southerners resulted in full-scale warfare. The Sudan gained its independence from Britain in 1956. As a part of the agreement, the southern Sudan which was mainly inhabited by either Nilotes or Bantu was attached to the new state despite the fact that it had been generally administered by the British authorities in Uganda whose peoples were closely akin to those in the Sudan. The attempts by a succession of Muslim northerners to rule the far distant south from Khartoum created a number of very serious problems for the southerners. When their petitions for redress went unanswered some of the more dissatisfied people turned to violence. Thus began a civil war which lasted for almost fifteen years. It was ended only in 1972 when the Sudan government granted the south near independence in deciding local issues.

The most recent example of near anarchy brought on by the vast differences between north and south was the war in Chad. Rebels in the north and east began in 1967 the long drawn-out struggle against President Tombalbaye and his southern-dominated government. Despite the presence of over 2,000 French troops sent by the request of the government, the rebels had total control of much of the country by the mid-1970s. In 1975 the southern-controlled government capitulated to the Muslim-dominated, Libyan-supported Liberation Front. Schisms with the Liberation Front prolonged the fighting for another five years, depopulating a large part of southern Chad and destroying its capital and largest city. Although many factors were involved in this bloody war, the major initial cause was the racial, religious, and economic differences between the north and south.

Even in states where the differences between ethnic, religious, or cultural groups have not resulted in warfare, there have been deep political and economic divisions which have generally resulted in instability. This instability has then reduced the chances for representative government to meet the many challenges and thus provided an excuse for the military to take control. Benin (Dahomey), Uganda, Upper Volta, Togo, Mali, and the Central African Republic are states whose recent history is illustrative of this generalization. Benin in the 1960s had a number of military coups directed against civilian governments which could not compromise the differences between various tribal and religious groups. Each time the military handed back control of the government to civilians, one or more of the political leaders would redirect government policy toward favoring a specific group and this in turn brought the military to intervene once again.

Uganda is another tragic illustration of the detrimental effects that local loyalties have on a central government. The British had ruled Uganda as a type of loose federation and recognized the particularistic complex cultures and political systems of the Nyoro, Ganda, Ankole, and Toro peoples. The ruler of each of these was treated in many ways as if he were in fact king over his people. The only loyalties to a central authority were those demanded by the British governmental system. The most powerful of the interlacustrine kings was the Kabaka of Buganda. In the 1950s when the British began to prepare all of Uganda for independence, they discovered that the Kabaka and his people did not wish to be a part of a larger polity. They pointed to their agreement of 1900 with the British and demanded that Buganda be recognized as independent. This crisis was temporarily ended only by the British exerting their police power and banishing the Kabaka. The affair did not end there since the centralized government of independent Uganda still had to deal with the Ganda who did not want to be governed by non-Ganda officials. Prime Minister Obote once again used military power to overawe the dissident kingdom. The necessity to balance the desires of the other differing peoples of Uganda presented a corollary problem which Obote's government could never solve. The military coup which overthrew his government brought to power General Idi Amin whose nine year tenure came to symbolize African misrule. Amin, a Muslim from a smaller northern group, favored those tribal segments and struck out against the more powerful sub-groups within the country. The governments since April 1979 when Amin fled Uganda have all been weak and again plagued by national divisions.

At this juncture the role of Asians in East and South Africa and the Lebanese and Syrians in West Africa should be mentioned briefly. The highly divergent group known as Asians came first to the Indian Ocean littoral in great numbers in the latter nineteenth century. Their frugality, hard work, and business sense combined with a sense of community brought many of them prosperity by the end of World War II. Most of the Asians were merchants and traders and came to occupy the mid-range positions in the mercantile establishments of Uganda, Kenya, and Tanzania. In South Africa their history was somewhat different but there, too, they prospered in business. Most of the Asian population there is concentrated in the coastal towns and cities of Natal. Friction between Africans and Asians has a long history. Asian merchants dealt directly with poor tribal Africans and many times the latter claimed to be cheated. Periodically there was violence between the groups. The worst early race riots in South Africa were between Asians and Africans in Durban. What to do with the very large, prosperous, and educated Asian population in South Africa remains one of the thorny problems confronting the apartheid committed white government of the republic.

The Asians were relatively well protected by the British during their tenure of power in East Africa, but as soon as independence was gained, African governments wanted to dislodge the Asians from their favored positions to make way for economically upward mobile Africans. Kenya and Tanzania have each taken differing approaches to their economy but both have sought by legal means to erode the position of the Asians. Tanzania because of its overall socialistic policy has been the more successful of the two, but each state still has a very large Asian community. Idi Amin of Uganda attacked the problem with his usual lack of understanding and finesse. In 1972 he simply ordered the entire Asian population of approximately 60,000 to leave the country. Although he solved the problem of the Asian minority living in Uganda, his actions directed against them went far toward ruining the economy of Uganda.

Lebanese and Syrians posed some of the same problems for many West African states as did the Asians on the other side of the continent. Concentrated generally in the cities and large towns, they controlled a large part of the direct trade with Africans. They also worked very hard, invested wisely, and in general could out-compete their African competitors. A series of serious problems was created for the newly independent governments in the 1960s wherever there was a large concentration of Middle Eastern merchants. However, over the past twenty years their numbers and influence have been minimized by legislation directed against alien entrepreneurs and in some cases by the nationalization of many businesses. There are still large Lebanese and Syrian populations resident in some West African states and they are still considered by some Africans as a threat to the economic well-being of a country.

The last group of Africans to consider in some detail are the European settlers. As noted previously, there were only a few areas in Africa where Europeans colonized in considerable numbers. In every area of sub-Saharan Africa where there was a large white population with the exception of the Republic of South Africa there has recently been large-scale warfare before the question of white or black dominance was answered. The reasons for this violence are obvious. Whites held a favored economic and political position in each territory before "the winds of change" began to blow across sub-Saharan Africa. They wished to retain their power for as long as possible, fearing the chaos that might follow if the majority Africans gained control of the government. In Kenya the bloodletting was relatively minor and the Mau Mau movement as an ongoing force was ended by the mid-1950s. In the half-decade following the end of the emergency in Kenya the British government abandoned complete support of the white colonists and the African majority was vested with control of the independent government in 1963. The policies of President Jomo Kenyatta's government after independence were such that the exodus of whites from the country was checked and a large number chose to remain to lend their specialized skills to the new state.

Elsewhere the contest for power between black and white was resolved only by long, drawn-out, bitter civil wars. The Portuguese government fearing the economic results of liberalization of policies toward its Africans territories attempted to hold them by force. On the other side, African liberation movements in Portuguese Guinea, Angola, and Mozambique took to the back country, organized guerrilla armies, and supported by most of the Africans, launched a series of attacks upon the Portuguese strongpoints. Despite the presence in Africa of over 100,000 men and modern sophisticated equipment, the task of reconquest proved too great for Portugal. In 1974 a new, more liberal Portuguese government recognized the impossibility of holding on to its empire and capitulated to the liberation movements. In each formerly dependent area the Africans organized governments which were ideologically counter to the old Portuguese system. Thus Portugal's struggle with its Africans subjects cost hundreds of millions of dollars, thousands of lives, and left a legacy of bitterness between white and black which will take decades to heal. The withdrawal of the Portuguese from Angola has resulted in an ongoing struggle for power between revolutionary groups. However, the transition in Mozambique and Portuguese Guinea went smoothly. There was a further price which each area had to pay. In the wake of the wars and peace settlements most of the white settlers left Angola and Mozambique. They took with them the bulk of the managerial expertise. Almost all the doctors, teachers, engineers, and trained technicians were white. The postwar penalty paid can be seen in comparative health, educational, and economic statistics from each of these areas.

Zimbabwe (Rhodesia) presents something of a similar story. The quarter-million whites who dominated every facet of life in the region then called Southern Rhodesia rebelled at the idea of accepting the British solution to the multiracial problem and in 1965 declared the area independent of British control. For the next fourteen years the white political leaders headed by Prime Minister Ian Smith maintained intact the economic and political system of Rhodesia despite condemnation by the British government and most countries in the United Nations. That independence was bought at an ever-increasing price as African liberation movements from their sanctuaries in Zambia and Mozambique struck with greater frequency across the borders. The cost in lives and property and increasing pressure from the United States, Britain, and South Africa finally forced the white regime to compromise. The extremely complex negotiations leading to a cessation of the guerrilla war lasted for over a year but finally the white minority surrendered their favored position and an African government was elected headed by Robert Mugabe, one of the guerrilla leaders. It is too early to have any certainty about the future of Zimbabwe but Mugabe has abandoned much of his previous revolutionary rhetoric and has attempted to follow the earlier example of Kenya in appealing to the white colonists to close off the past, trust his government, and remain in the country. Zimbabwe can ill afford the loss of the most educated and talented segment of its society.

The recent changes in the government of Zimbabwe leave only one area in Africa where major black-white confrontations are likely. The Republic of South Africa has been the bastion of white supremacy throughout the twentieth century and most particularly since the Nationalist Party election victory of 1948. Since then a succession of different prime ministers have not wavered from the policy of apartheid. The basic structure of separation was laid down in the 1950s and still dominates government thinking. The fundamental goal of apartheid is separation. Bantu and white are to have different rules governing housing, labor contracts, social contacts, and access to government. At the same time South Africa's burgeoning economy demands more Bantu unskilled and semiskilled workers in the urban areas. This dilemma has been temporarily resolved by creating a homelands policy where a Bantu is assigned only one area where he can have full rights. No major city is included. All Bantu, no matter what their length of residence in a city, are considered to be temporary and can be removed at any time.

The ultimate goal of the government's homelands policy is to create all white and all black areas. These different regions could then be loosely associated in a federal form of government. As an interim arrangement, the homelands would be given their political independence from the republic. So far the Transkei, Bophutatswana, and Venda have all been declared independent, have had elections for their governments, and are considered to have been politically separated from South Africa. None of these states have been recognized by the world community, most critics pointing to the economic nonviability of the enclaves and the continued domination of all aspects of life in the new polities by the white government at Pretoria.

The most pressing problems for the Nationalist government is the continued increase in the size of the urban Bantu work force and their growing politicalization. A series of disturbances in the Bantu areas adjacent to the major cities in the latter 1970s indicates the revolutionary potential of the millions of hitherto unorganized, "temporary" inhabitants of Bantu townships such as Soweto adjacent to Johannesburg. However, the South African army and police are well trained and equipped and have so far been able to contain all the spontaneous movements. One reason for their success is the government's ability to keep a leadership cadre from gaining appreciable influence over the Bantu communities.

Apartheid has succeeded in South Africa despite the vigorous opposition of a large sector of the white community. In the years immediately after 1948 most whites of British descent concurred in their hostility toward apartheid. With time their opposition has faltered. In each major election the majority won by the pro-apartheid National Part has increased. The British moderates and liberals no longer have any but the most minimal influence over Parliament. It seems likely that this erosion of white opposition will continue since the governments of Prime Ministers Vorster and Botha have begun to remove parts of the apartheid system which dealt with personal relations between the races. Botha has been particularly concerned to do away with "petit-apartheid" in order to create a better environment for cooperation. However, it would be a mistake to believe that his government is abandoning the central core of the apartheid system.

One of the strongest arguments made by the advocates of apartheid is that the Bantu in South Africa are not a single people. Rather they are deeply divided linguistically and historically from one another. There are many Bantu nations belonging either to the Sotho or Nguni subgroups. The Tswana, Xosa, Pondo, Tembu, and Zulu are indeed different people, as different from one another in many cases as European nations. They speak different languages, have different traditions, and in some cases have a long history of hatred toward one another. Numbers of people are also an important consideration since most of these people do not belong to "tribal" units. The Xosa and Zulu each claiming almost four million persons are nations and the attitudes and specific goals of each can be very different. Thus even discounting the considerable Indian and Colored population, South Africa is a complex amalgam of African peoples with political and economic problems not too much different from the states north of the Limpopo.

An adjunct problem to apartheid in South Africa is the question of Namibia. Formerly called South-West Africa, it was seized by Germany during the "scramble," taken from them in 1915, and administered by South Africa as a mandate of the League of Nations after World War I. The question of sovereignty which has agitated South Africa and the United Nations is too complicated to recount here. It is sufficient to say that one of the major problems concerns an extension of apartheid into the area and the domination of the political and economic life of the region by white settlers. Corollary problems arise from the great divisions in the nonwhite population. There are Bantu agriculturalists and herders such as the Herero and the Ovambo, remnant groups of Hottentots (Khoi), and wandering bands of Bushmen (San). The claim of the most active African political group in Namibia, SWAPO, that it speaks for all Africans in the areas, is contested not only by whites, but also by some of the leaders of the other clan and tribal units.

Before closing this brief description of the manifold problems caused by the deep divisions among Africa's peoples, the group which has had the most influence on Africa since World War II should be surveyed. This is the ever-growing number of Western-educated Africans. In all African territories before independence there were very few persons who could claim even the equivalent of secondary educations. The numbers of university graduates even in the most advanced states such as Nigeria, Kenya, and Senegal were miniscule. Yet this was the group to which the imperial powers turned at independence. Their small numbers and lack of experience in governing have been one reason for the political instability of Africa. In the past two decades every African state has spent a large portion of its income on education. There are dozens of universities in Africa and many thousands of students studying in Europe and the United States. It would be sanguine to imagine that these better educated and trained Africans will be able to solve quickly the continent's manifold problems. However, there are some hopeful signs. There is a general unity among these educated Africans because of their shared educational experiences. They are the ones who believe most strongly in such ideals as freedom, representative government, and cooperation between states. Whether from Gambia, Nigeria, Kenya, or Zambia, these young men and women share a common language and a common set of European philosophical and scientific values. The same comment can be made of the elites in Francophone Africa. The partial unity of this most important segment of Africa's new generations may in time go far toward healing many of the centuries-old divisions between the various African national and tribal groups of this complex continent.

FOUR
Agricultural Limitations

The many and rapid changes which have occurred in Africa during the twentieth century have not altered the salient fact that the majority of the continent's people still earn their sustenance from either herding or farming. Most of Africa's independent governments have been reluctant to recognize this central fact, preferring instead to expend large sums of money upon prestigious projects which the leaders believed might aid in industrializing their states. However, concern with the health of the agricultural sector has recently been growing even in the most prosperous African nations. During the past decade more money has been expended upon agricultural development than ever before and yet there has generally not been enough improvement in production to offset the growth in population. The reasons for the crisis in African agriculture are many and will vary from one area to another. These will be more easily understood if one subdivides agricultural pursuits into three segments and surveys each separately. These subdivisions are pastoralism, traditional agriculture, and export agriculture.

Across the wide semi-arid reaches of Africa's dry savannah lands where the annual rainfall does not exceed twenty inches the chief occupation of the inhabitants is animal husbandry. In those regions immediately adjacent to the Sahara Desert the prized animal is the camel which provides both transport and food to the many differing nomadic living groups. In the regions of better grass and more available water, cattle herding is the chief support of most of the people. Almost all Caucasian and Negro pastoralists also keep large herds of sheep and goats. The major concern of pastoralists of all types is the availability of water, and some groups such as the Fula and Tucolor in western Africa specialize in animal husbandry and have developed complex systems of migrations based upon seasonal rainfall patterns. However, most sudanic groups give their cattle little care since they are viewed more as a visible sign of wealth rather than an economic asset.

During the past twenty years two major natural events have threatened the lifestyles of most of the savannah pastoralists who live in the northern hemisphere. The first was lack of rainfall. Beginning in the mid-1960s, the amount of rain which fell in the Sahel zone stretching from Mauritania to Ethiopia decreased drastically. Pastoralists in this vast region depended almost exclusively upon the seasonal rains since the various governments had expended little money on wells, dams, or catchment areas. Denied normal amounts of rainfall for over seven years, most of the livestock of all types died. It has been estimated that in only the year 1973 over 3.5 million cattle worth approximately $400 million perished. The human loss was also very great. An estimated 100,000 people starved to death in the affected area of Ethiopia alone and uncounted thousands perished in other Sahel states. This widespread starvation occurred despite the considerable aid which was funneled into the Sahel by affluent governments touched by the tragedy of mass starvation. The United States provided the bulk of relief food which totaled over $150 million in grain shipments alone.

Deprived of their camel or cattle herds, many of the survivors could do nothing but remain in the temporary relief camps which had been established adjacent to the major towns. By the mid-1970s over 5 million persons were refugees in the crowded camps and towns. Many of the nomads of the Sahel and desert regions such as the Tuareg lost a way of life and have become wards of the government in an alien town or sedentary agricultural village environment. The states most affected by the drought were Mali, Niger, Chad, and Ethiopia, but no region in the Sahel escaped. The governments of Niger and Ethiopia were overthrown largely because of their inability to cope with the massive relief efforts necessary to feed their starving people. By 1975 the annual rainfall had returned to normal levels and the more fortunate of the pastoralists once again took up their old patterns of life. However, beginning in 1979 the average precipitation started to decline and the Sahel regions are once again threatened with a major drought.

There is little which can be done for the savannah peoples if they are once again confronted by a succession of drought years. The cost of building water retention systems is so great that only a few African states can afford them. Although the earlier drought sent a warning to all the Sahel polities, the time has been too short to see what a positive effect that the water conservation efforts of richer states such as Nigeria will be. The military and civilian governments of Nigeria have spent considerable sums on wells, bore holes, small and large dams, and local irrigation projects throughout the northern regions. Without such massive efforts as those of Nigeria, droughts will continue to bring starvation and death to the pastoral peoples of the savannah. If the present weather pattern continues, the pastoral way of life for millions of persons will be brought to an end.

The second natural event which deeply affects pastoral peoples is the continued transformation of savannah lands into desert. In some parts of West Africa this transformation is proceeding at the rate of thirty miles per year. Obviously the lack of rainfall over extended periods is a major contributing factor to this dessication. However, the people themselves are also guilty of practices which ultimately can mean the ruination of once viable pasture lands. Overgrazing is one evil which is not even recognized as a problem by most herders. In many societies possession of many animals, particularly cattle, is a sign of the wealth and prestige of the owner. Animals then are not just a source of food or a means of making money. They are an index to one's position within his clan or tribe. The condition or quality of the cattle is not necessarily important in determining the size of herds.

A major limitation to the substantial improvement of cattle herds in Africa is the presence of differing varieties of tse-tse flies in many regions which would otherwise provide good grazing land. The flies are carriers of forms of sleeping sickness which are usually not fatal to man, but can be devastating to other warm-blooded animals. Many African herders understand the life cycle of the fly and move their herds from one place to another in regions that normally would not be considered safe for cattle. Such activity is a local phenomenon; most tse-tse fly infested regions are closed to the herders. African cattle breeders in some of the savannah areas have various strains of cattle which over the centuries have developed an immunity to sleeping sickness. These cattle are normally small and give very little milk. Early attempts to improve African cattle by crossbreeding with European varieties generally ended in failure. European beef and dairy cattle can survive only in the tse-tse free plains areas or in the highlands.

The problem of unchecked multiplication of large cattle herds is particularly acute among some Nilotic and Bantu peoples who live in the savannah lands of eastern and southern Africa.

One reason for the denuding of the land in the Transkei and Zululand regions of the Republic of South Africa is the size of the cattle herds kept by the Xosa and Zulu. The problem is not as dramatic among other Sotho and Nguni, but it exists in all of these cattle herding societies. One of the best examples of the devastating effect of overgrazing can be observed in southern Kenya where the picturesque Masai clans live. The Masai more than any other people of Africa base their society upon the cow. They believe that their great god gave all the cattle in the world to the Masai for safekeeping. It is a task imposed upon them. Any other type of work until quite recently was unthinkable for a Masai. They follow their age-old methods of caring for the cattle and are, in many ways, quite adept. However, they have resisted all attempts at such modern management techniques as limitation of herds and selective breeding. One reason for their resistance has been the logic of the new systems which would require them to settle in one place near wells or catchment areas and begin to diversify their economy by also planting crops. This they have refused to do. The weather conditions which were so disastrous for the western Sahel also struck Kenya in the 1970s. The results are there for all to see. Large sections of southern Kenya have become wastelands where not even the most hardy antelope will venture. During most of the year there is no grass and some Masai cattle have become browsers. Masai herdsmen will pull over the tops of thorn trees so their cattle will be able to eat the leaves from the trees. In other areas the ever increasing Masai cattle herds are in open competition with wild grazers, and more and more the antelope, zebra, and wildebeestes are being restricted in their food gathering.

The problem of southern Kenya and other similar although not as extreme cases are known to the individual governments concerned. However, in each state, dictating change to a particular subgroup such as the Masai could be extremely unpopular and fraught with serious political consequences. Thus as with population control, the expedient course of action for governments is simply to ignore what goes on. This attitude applies to control of the vast numbers of goats kept by almost all savannah dwellers. Some better idea of this tragi-comedy goat problem can be gained by noting that according to the best estimates, there were over 6 million goats in each of three West African states— Mauritania, Mali, and Niger. The goat is a perfect animal for such harsh environments. It can be left to fend for itself and its digestive system will allow it to eat almost anything. Goats, however, do untold damage to their environment because of their grazing and browsing habits. In some locales the trees appear as if they have been trimmed by a meticulous gardner just to the height that goats can reach. Some African political leaders have recognized how destructive goat herds are, but are unable to do anything positive to restrict their possession or limit the numbers. Goats have been kept by Africans for generations. They are a part of the life of agricultural and pastoral villages and they do provide a ready source of food for the protein deficient people of the savannah. The only limiting factor on the numbers and depradations of goats appear to be a natural one. Some of the vulnerable grassy savannah will gradually become more arid and will not support an increased human or animal population. This dessication is merely speeded up by the continuation of the recent drought conditions.

Taking into account local political and societal differences between pastoral groups, there appear to be only a few viable solutions to the questions raised by the over-population of animals and man in the savannah. Obviously the key is making available a secure water supply for the herders and their animals. In many places this will be very hard to achieve due to the nature of the earth's substratum over broad areas. The best that can be hoped for in such places is to create catchment areas so that most of the rainfall is not lost. In other regions where there is a shallow water table, wells can be sunk and permanent oases can be created. As noted before, such projects are expensive and beyond the capacity of many of the impoverished governments of the savannah.

Another costly set of projects correlate with water development are schemes to halt the intrusion of the desert. To achieve this, hardy native trees must be planted and the affected regions resown with native or foreign grasses. Hopefully in time this new vegetation could reverse the present conversion of grazing land to desert. If any plan is to succeed the very conservative pastoralists must accept the realities of their changed situation. The fundamental change in their lifestyle would be the necessity to settle in one place where water is readily available and thus abandon their age-old practice of wandering. This is perhaps the most difficult task because no people are eager to give up a way of life which has satisfied their progenitors for centuries.

Without being didactic, it does appear that if African herders are to prosper, they must learn modern Western techniques of cattle breeding. This, too, implies a basic change in their attitudes toward their herds. Mere numbers of cattle should not be the measure of a successful cattleman. Quality of the herd should be more important. There are a number of places in Africa where valid comparisons can be made between traditional and Western ideas of animal husbandry. In Kenya there are a number of whites who chose to remain after independence and who own cattle ranches. Some of these ranches are very large and efficiently managed. The owners have inbred various subtypes of African cattle to provide a relatively standard, large healthy breed. These cattle are generally grass fed just as the herds of their Masai neighbors, but they are not allowed to overgraze. The numbers of cattle per acre are strictly limited and herds are shifted from one area to another in order to allow the grass in a given locale to recover from grazing. These relatively simple procedures produce large herds of excellent cattle which bring premium market prices. By contrast, the Masai cattle are indeed poor creatures with only a minimal market value. Even more important, the conservation techniques utilized on the large, modern Western style ranches have preserved the land while whole sections of the Masai reserve grow ever less productive.

One other area of comparison is southern Africa. In both the Republic of South Africa and Zimbabwe, cattle are important to both black and white settlers. Here in both highland and lowland regions one can again compare quality and productivity of herds and the effects these cattle have on the environment. In both regions the traditional sector provides only a small portion of exported meat. In the more healthy regions, white ranchers have imported quality European cattle and follow standardized modern techniques for their care. Almost all dairy farming in both states is controlled by the white community. The lessons of all the southern regions seem apparent although carrying out the imperatives of these might be very difficult. If pastoralism is to continue as a viable way of life, basic modifications should be made in the traditional view of cattle herding. As land becomes more scarce, Africans must take better care of their grazing and water resources. Herds must be reduced in size to meet reasonable grazing standards and every effort should be made to upgrade their quality. Whenever possible those techniques which have made Western ranchers so successful should be adopted either totally or in a modified form by the African cattle herders. Failing some major effort by various governments in conjunction with the cooperation of the peoples involved to achieve better management, the African environmental situation can only get worse. The dessication of pastoral land colored by the omnipresence of drought makes the future of Africa's savannah reaches particularly dark.

The many problems of traditional argiculturists throughout the continent, although not as desperate as those facing the pastoralists of the savannah, are nevertheless very serious and complex. Unless African governments and the traditional farmers confront them soon, the entire economy of some sub-Saharan states could collapse. There are certain general factors which should be borne in mind before discussing the specifics of any region. The first has already been discussed in some detail and involves the quality of agricultural land. Most land in Africa is marginal and needs to be treated with care. The second point to stress is the epidemic overpopulation which creates unprecedented pressures to overexploit the available land. The third fact is the innate conservatism of the African farmer. He has a set methodology which has functioned for his group for generations and he will resist most changes however logical they may appear to the reformer. The last factor is poverty. The traditional farmer, no matter where he labors in Africa, has little or no capital. Even if he wished, he could not undertake by himself even the most basic steps toward improving the yields on his lands.

Landholding in the Western world is based upon the principle of freehold. A man purchases land and that land, subject to minor regulations, is his to do with as he wishes. African landholding, except in a minority of cases, is not freehold. One finds freehold land in the towns and cities, in areas of reclaimed land, or where public land has been sold or where Europeans had once lived. However, most African societies consider land to be held either directly by the community or to be used by the individual farmer for the good of that community. Many African groups believe, like the Kikuyu of Kenya, that the land is sacred and given in trust to all the people. It can be subdivided or sold only by an action of either the community as a whole or of their representatives. Other African societies, as with the clan-oriented Ibo of eastern Nigeria, allow the individual to hold and use land as if it were his own, subject to the overall control exercised by the clan leaders.

Communal landholding of any type has at least two fundamental consequences. The first is obvious. Transfers of land must meet not just the approval of individual farmers, but the community as a whole. In most African agricultural societies the village and clan leaders are old men and very conservative. They would view with suspicion any requests by more progressive farmers to increase allotments of land or any other modifications which might lead to greater production. This is one reason why African governments have had to take an active role in modernization. Government agents bring pressures to bear upon a village head or his council which may in time change their attitudes toward modernization.

The second consequence of communal landholding has been the assignment of lands to individuals based upon the needs of the nuclear or extended family. This normally was not done in a systematic fashion and therefore over the generations, noncontiguous small-plot landholding has become the pattern. In the past such a truncation of village or clan lands mattered little since the plots, however scattered, were sufficient for the farmers to grow those crops which could keep a family alive. This system, given the pressures of the modern age, is highly inefficient. It is uneconomical for a village, let alone an individual, to expend money for farm implements which are designed to be used on larger farms. The glib answer to both these problems is that African villages must adopt a new method of land allocation which will permit the use of more sophisticated equipment and perhaps planting of a larger variety of crops not only for sustenance, but profit. To do this in any given locale will require persuasion and pressure by government agents and the very conservative people must be given time to accustom themselves to the changes. The most successful approach to solving the problems of consolidation of land has been the establishment of cooperatives. The exact nature of these varies from place to place, but the general outlines are similar. The directorate of the cooperative is normally composed of representatives from the traditional leadership of the village or clan, and agents from the agriculture department or some other specialized agency. Decisions are made for better utilization of the land, what crops are more profitable for planting, and whether the group needs newer, better tools. In most areas the cooperative also acts as a buying agent purchasing seeds, fertilizers, and tools in bulk and buying the surplus crops from the farmers for sale elsewhere. The cooperative system is thus a compromise between the old and new.

Some governments have attempted to expand the cooperative concept into a standardized national system. Sekou Touré and associates in Guinea have slowly implemented their integrative plans for agriculture. After an initial period of lowered production Guinea's agricultural output of basic foodstuffs has increased considerably. One must bear in mind that the reforms of agriculture in Guinea are but a part of a total package which the party leaders have designed and implemented to make Guinea a socialist state. The mineral wealth of Guinea has paradoxically provided the government with the funds to carry out their agricultural reforms. Thus plans for improvement of traditional farming methods which might work in Guinea are not necessarily transferable to other African polities.

Tanzania's program has been the most publicized agricultural reform in Africa. President Julius Nyerere announced to the world that agriculture was to be Tanzania's first priority soon after the ruling party's decision in 1967 to make Tanzania a socialist state. It was an obvious move since Tanzania is one of the poorer East African states with few mineral resources and a growing deficit caused partially by the need to import food. The government's solution was designed to be a return to genuine cooperation between government and villagers in what was called the *ujamaa* program. The idea was deceptively simple. Villagers would work in conjunction with government agents to increase the supply of foodstuffs. In the main, traditional methods were to be used, thus reducing the need for expensive machinery. The government was also to create new villages and encourage city dwellers to move back to the farms or aid in the planting and harvesting of crops. The plan has been in operation in some parts of Tanzania for almost a decade and the reports on its success are contradictory. In some areas it is obvious that agricultural output has been increased. In many other regions it appears not to be working. There are several reasons given for the program's failure in these areas. The most important seems to be the role of the government bureaucracy. The government attempted to standardize methods and then these were imposed upon the village or clan leaders. Such centralized decision making led traditional leaders only to support the reforms to the extent they felt necessary to keep government agents from imposing further upon them. The most necessary ingredient for the success of any agricultural reform, the full cooperation of the traditional farmers, has thus been lost in much of the rural area. Despite the shortcomings of the actual reform program in Tanzania, one thing at least has been accomplished. Officials at the highest level have recognized the central role of agriculture in the functioning of the state and made its improvement the first charge on government activity.

Problems related to cash crops must also be considered within the context of traditional subsistence agriculture because there is such an overlapping of production. Only in the poorest areas of Africa or during drought periods does one find a totally subsistence agriculture. Long before the imperial period of the twentieth century there were thriving local markets where farmers could exchange surpluses. There were also marjor markets in the larger towns and cities, key links in long distance trade, where nonperishable items could be bought and sold. Among many African societies women played a most important role in the local exchange. The Fante, Yoruba, Ibo, Ibibio, and many other African societies held women responsible for growing the food necessary to maintain their families. Any surplus belonged to them and could be sold and the profits kept. Many of the market women in West Africa built their fortunes from the few pennies profit they could make in local trading.

There were many difficulties in the way of traditional farmers increasing the volume of surplus food to trade. In the past there was no way of preserving many types of crops, and this restricted the planting of any more of these foodstuffs than could be used locally. Much of the surplus food trade was controlled by women who had specific duties in their villages and to their families. Thus they could normally not engage in trade very far from home. The building of roads into most of the bush areas in the twentieth century has extended the range of market activities, but not enough so that one can expect local surpluses in one area to be transferred easily to another poorer region. It is much more likely that farmers will continue to restrict their seasonal production to meet only local demands.

During the mid-nineteenth century European traders concerned with their loss of profits because of the demise of the slave trade discovered a few items which had ready markets in Europe. At first the most important of these products were palm oil and rubber. A few years later it was discovered that peanuts thrived in the sandy soil of parts of the savannah and that cocoa and coffee also could be grown profitably in certain areas. The introduction of such crops marked the beginnings of Africa's export agriculture. Many of the crops introduced to Africa in the twentieth century were considered to be plantation crops. Large sections of land generally owned or leased by Europeans were devoted to their cultivation. During the imperial period some African areas became almost totally dependent upon one or two of these crops. Extensive rubber plantations financed by Firestone Rubber Company bolstered the faltering economy of Liberia, oil palm plantations were scattered throughout Zaire, and coffee and tea were extensively cultivated in the Ivory Coast, Uganda, Kenya, Zaire, and Tanzania, and sisal became a major plantation crop for much of coastal East Africa.

Many of the export crops were not only produced by European agro-business interests, but also by African entrepreneurs. Almost all of the peanuts exported from Senegal, the Gambia, and Nigeria were produced by African small holders. The same was also true of the production of cocoa and coffee in the Ivory Coast, Ghana, and Nigeria, cotton in the Sudan, and the collection of oil palm products in eastern Nigeria and the Cameroons. Even where the bulk of an export crop was at first controlled by European firms, the prospect of profits encouraged many Africans to undertake its cultivation. For example, in the coastal regions of Liberia, the Firestone experiment led to much African investment in small size rubber plantations. By the early 1960s most states were largely supported by a few crops which were in great demand throughout the world. Since World War II there has been a strenuous attempt by all African governments to upgrade the quality of their exports so they would be competitive on the world market. Despite all the attempts to increase the acreage under cultivation and the quality of the product, there has been a distinct falling off in African exports over the past decade which has created major financial problems for the governments involved.

There are many reasons for the shortfall in agricultural production throughout Africa. All exporting states are at the mercy of world demand and price structures which are beyond the control either of the producer or his government. There have been great fluctuations in the market price of most of the export commodities produced in Africa. The creation of marketing boards in the 1960s helped to stabilize markets to a certain extent, but even states who belong to international marketing agencies for products such as coffee and cocoa have not been completely successful in maintaining stable prices. The cost of all items needed in producing the cash crops has increased drastically during the past decade, especially petroleum-based items. This factor, combined with falling prices, has in many areas put a curb upon expansion of acreage or improvement of product. An increasing and shifting population also has had an effect upon exports. Northern Nigeria was once a major exporter of peanuts, peanut oil, and oil cake, and the income the state received from these exports was considerable. The increased population of the country has created such a demand for oil that hardly any is now sold outside Nigeria.

France for years maintained a price support system for specified products in its empire. These supports were continued after the independence of the constituent states. In Senegal, for example, peanut farmers could expect a guaranteed price per ton for their peanut products which at times exceeded the world market price. The French removed those supports just as the drought hit the Sahel regions. The combination of lowered prices, inflation, and drought forced many farmers to give up planting peanuts and instead content themselves with only food crops. The government of Senegal for over a hundred years has depended upon the peanut crop. Thus the falling off of exports has had a very detrimental effect upon government services. One should also note that it is doubtful whether Senegal or even Nigeria could have continued to dominate a large share of the world's market for peanuts. Competition from other producing states even before the drought had already cut heavily into the markets once believed secure. Peanut growers in the United States could produce so much more of higher quality peanut products and could sell them at lower margins of profit than any African distributor.

Other factors have had a great impact upon the productivity of export crops in certain regions. Political instability which seems epidemic in Africa has had a devastating effect upon agriculture. Uganda, parts of which were once believed by the early British explorers to contain the most productive lands of East Africa, is now a near disaster area. During the period of misrule of Idi Amin, production lagged, distribution systems were allowed to decay, and finally civil war interrupted the planting and harvesting cycles. Zaire, despite its mineral riches and diversified agriculture, has never totally recovered from the five year turmoil of the early 1960s. The export figures for the past decade for Angola and Mozambique show clearly the devastating effect of their wars of liberation upon the agricultural sector. Eastern Nigeria, the site of the three year Biafran War, had its oil palm industry shattered and it has never recovered. Zimbabwe escaped relatively unscathed from the decade-old guerrilla war because its export agriculture was controlled by whites, most of whose farms were located away from the actual fighting. It is much too early to say what effect the recent change in government will have upon Zimbabwe's healthy heterogeneous agricultural system. If the endemic fighting between the two rival African parties continues, then both traditional and export agriculture will suffer.

Lack of capital, conservative landholding policies, and political instability are all major factors in restricting the development of export agriculture by entrepreneurs in most African regions. Thus the governments have had to assume a more prominent role in attempting to improve agricultural productivity than would be the case in Western Europe or the United States. The states of Africa which have been most successful in maintaining a healthy, growing export agriculture have certain things in common. Much can be learned about the potential for development if one isolates three of these states and investigates specifically why they have been successful when schemes for agricultural improvement in most African territories have been disastrous.

The Sudan, largest state in Africa, has a great variety of land forms, climatic zones, and many differing peoples and societies. Except in the few towns, agriculture is the major occupation of most Sudanese. Traditional methods of agriculture are practiced throughout most of the country. In the far west the farmers terrace the hills of the Jebel Marra. This is also done in parts of the Nubian Mountains in Kordofan. On these terraces and in the valleys they plant garden vegetables, cotton, and tobacco. Farming is much better in the savannah areas, where the annual rainfall is between 12 to 30 inches, than in any other parts of the country. This broad section includes the provinces of Southern Darfur, Kordofan, the Blue Nile, and portions of Kassala. Here the basic crops are millet, maize, sesame, peanuts, tobacco, and cotton. In many parts of the Kordofan the inhabitants practice both sedentary agriculture and pastoralism. Another area of intensive, traditional-style agriculture is along the narrow strip adjacent to the Nile which extends over 1,000 miles from Khartoum to the Egyptian border. This fertile belt of land never exceeds three miles in width and yet it supports over three-quarters of a million persons. Most farmers earn their livelihood from growing millet, wheat, garden crops, and harvesting the date palms. In the far southern provinces, Bantu agriculturists retrieve their land from the bush by a combination of clearing methods including burning. The grain and garden products they grow are used mainly by the producers or find their way into local markets. The south contributes very little that is exportable to the Sudanese economy.

The foundation of Sudan's economy is irrigated agriculture of a variety of crops, the most important of which is cotton. Natural or flush irrigation is used in the Tokar River delta where over 100,000 acres is under cultivation. More control is exercised over flooding in the Gash River delta northwest of Kassala where approximately 50,000 acres of rich soil are utilized to grow high grade cotton. There is also some flush irrigation in the Nubia Mountain area. However, the largest and most successful irrigation scheme is that of the Gezira. First conceived by the British who in 1925 constructed a dam across the Blue Nile at Sennar and completed most of the irrigation canals by 1930, the Gezira and the new Manigil extension now cover approximately 2 million acres. The main canal from the Sennar Dam is over one hundred miles long and runs parallel to the Blue Nile. From this, three major subsidiary canals and their branches run westward to service the lands under cultivation. Another large area upstream from the Gezira is also being developed. A new dam at Roseires, completed in 1966, has a water storage capacity twice that of Sennar. The new dam and canal system at this Rahad River scheme enabled over one-third million more acres to be brought under cultivation.

The building of the high dam at Aswan in Egypt caused Lake Nasser to flood large areas of the northern Sudan necessitating the resettlement of thousands of people. Most of them have been moved to an area along the Atbara River east of Khartoum. There the government constructed the Kashem el Girba Dam and brought over 400,000 acres under cultivation. Another cotton-growing scheme attempted by the British and continued by the independent Khartoum government was located in Equatoria and called the Zande Scheme. Its aim was to improve the economic conditions of the very poor southern Sudan. It failed because of lower market prices for cotton, internal competition, difficulty of transport, and the civil war.

The lands and equipment of the Gezira-Manigil, the Kashem el Girba, and the Rahad River are all nationalized. Production and distribution is planned and highly controlled. In the Gezira, for example, the cotton is grown by almost 100,000 tenants who farm plots varying in size from 15 to 40 acres. They are allowed to keep 40 percent of the profits from cotton and everything realized from other crops. In addition to the tenants, there is a very large labor force of approximately one-quarter million needed to produce the crops in the Gezira-Managil area alone. Each area is assigned a specific crop rotation scheme. In the Gezira region one-third of the area is normally planted to cotton. The rest of the cultivated land is planted in wheat and vegetables or left fallow. There are two large ginning plants located at Wad Medani which handle most of the cotton crop. In the Kashim el Girba, sugar cane is also grown and there is a sugar refining plant on the site. All planning, planting, and distribution on the nationalized lands of the Gezira region are controlled by the Sudan Gezira Board.

Much of the gross cultivation and spraying of the irrigated areas between the two Niles is done by mechanical means, but a great amount of the actual farming and irrigation is still done by relatively primitive handwork. Mechanized farming is also practiced in other parts of the Sudan. Outside of the Gezira the largest scheme is northwest of Gadoref and just south of Kassala. There over one and one-half million acres are planted in a variety of crops such as dura (a type of millet), peanuts, and cotton. These crops are rotated and a large part of the task of cultivation and harvesting is by means of tractors and other mechanical aids.

The Ivory Coast in many ways stands in stark contrast to the Sudan. It is smaller, tropical, and although diverse, its population is much more homogeneous than the Sudan. They do share certain common economic features. The French discovered in the early twentieth century that the climate and soils were excellent for two export crops—cocoa and coffee. French private capital flowed to the area, particularly in the years following World War I, and there developed a significant plantation-style agriculture in the immediate hinterland. The French government gave its support to these endeavors and the planters were guaranteed markets in France with relatively stable prices. Very soon as was the case in Ghana and Nigeria, African small holders began to emulate the European farmers. Although at first the government favored the French planters, they did not discourage Africans from gaining a share of the market. Government subsidies were also made available to them for tools, better strains of plants, and acquisition of land. The government also stressed the improvement of these cash crops in their efficient department of agriculture.

The stable government of the Ivory Coast has since independence continued and even broadened the supports given to the production of export crops. Far from driving out the Europeans, they have been encouraged to continue to invest in the future of the country. There are an estimated 50,000 French who live in the Ivory Coast. These residents and the French companies and banks, finding a congenial environment, have increased substantially the money available for investment in all segments of the economy. In the agricultural sector this has meant an ever-increasing profit for the farmers. The export of cocoa has been worth more than $130 million annually since 1970. Coffee is an even more valuable commodity, the Ivory Coast being the third largest producer of this important plantation crop. Over 80 percent of the coffee produced in the Ivory Coast is prima or superior grade beans. Almost as valuable as coffee and cocoa as a money earner is the export of timber, especially hardwood. Another crop which has in recent years become important is pineapple, the Ivory Coast having become the world's third largest producer.

Kenya is the third area to consider briefly in this all too general survey of states which have developed successful export agriculture. Before independence Kenya's agriculture was divided into two sectors. European farmers produced the bulk of Kenya's export crops. Coffee, tea, and sisal were produced by a minority of farmers generally in that most fertile area north and west of Nairobi called the "White Highlands." African agriculture was, in the main, confined to the production of foodstuffs for local consumption. Africans were actively discouraged from raising coffee or tea because it was felt that the quality of Kenya's exports would suffer if small holders began to market goods of inferior quality. Since independence the government has done a number of things to improve the quality and quantity of African agriculture. They intervened directly in clan disputes over land and discouraged the extreme fragmentation of communal lands which had made it difficult for African farmers, even with excellent land, to be productive. Large tracts of land were purchased from European farmers and redistributed to African small holders. By the end of the 1960s over 30,000 families had been resettled on 1.75 million acres. This policy, while satisfying the desire of

Africans to have land, was less productive of results since it broke up large economic units into small ones. Since 1970 the stress has been upon the *shirka* scheme whereby large units would be kept intact and a number of Africans who had been resettled would share in the work and the profits of these farms.

The results of these actions have been dramatic. Most of Kenya's small-scale farming is in subsistence crops such as maize, wheat, sorghum, millet, and rice. With advice on more efficient planting, better seeds, and fertilizers, the output per acre increased impressively during the years after 1965. Kenya's agriculture is diversified enough to provide for almost all the basic foodstuffs needed by the people, with surpluses left over to sell to neighboring areas. This is particularly true of maize and wheat. Better hybrid types of the former and more acres devoted to the latter crop has allowed a large amount of these staples to be marketed outside the areas of production.

It is in the area of export agriculture where the most important changes have occurred. In 1964 African farmers produced only 28 percent of the export crops; by 1973 they were responsible for over 55 percent. The most important cash crop is coffee, which is grown at altitudes between 5,000 and 6,000 feet north of Nairobi and on the slopes of Mt. Kenya and Mt. Elgon. Coffee was once grown only on large plantations, but there has been a shift in emphasis to the point where African small holders now produce the bulk of the crop. These farmers harvest their crop and sell it through one of the many cooperative societies. Prices, standards, and exports are handled by the Kenya Coffee Board. More than 70,000 tons of coffee, worth over $102 million, were exported in 1973. Tea is the second most valuable export and Kenya is Africa's leading producer. The tea plants are grown in the acid soils of the western highlands at elevations above 6,000 feet. Tea, like coffee in the past, was primarily a plantation crop. African small holders, however, with the encouragement of the Kenya Development Authority, now plant more acres than do the plantations and they produce over one-third of the total crop. Kenya exported 123 million pounds of tea in 1973 as compared to only 44 million pounds in 1964. The 1973 tea exports earned over $48 million.

Sisal, introduced to East Africa in the 1890s, is another important crop which is particularly suited for plantations. This is because the most economic way of using the sisal decorticating plant is on a year-round basis; therefore, large acreages must be planted to be harvested all year around. However, competition from synthetic fibers has caused considerable retraction in sisal production. In the period from 1965 to 1972 over two-thirds of the sisal plantations ceased operations in Kenya. By 1973 sisal accounted for only 5 percent of total exports as contrasted to twice that percentage a decade before. It is, nevertheless, still an important money earner, bringing in approximately $20 million in 1973. Pyrethrum, a plant with daisy-like flowers which when dried and processed provides chemicals for insecticides nontoxic to animals, has been growing in popularity. It is now grown in scattered locales throughout the western highlands, much of it by African small holders. Kenya provides approximately 70 percent of the world's supply of pyrethrum.

One should not be sanguine even about these three African states. The government and farmers of each area still face continuing problems if the current agricultural propserity of their states is to be maintained. Some of these such as overpopulation, the marginal quality of the soil, and lack of good conservation policies have already been alluded to. Other dangers beyond the control of any government would be the onset of disease such as swollen shoot in the cocoa plant which could destroy productivity of large areas, continuing inflation, and political disorder.

Despite their differences, an observer can note certain common features in each of these three prosperous states. The first factor is obvious. The export crop being produced should be in continuing demand throughout the world. There is no need to create a world market for such exports as cotton, coffee, cocoa, sisal, and pyrethrum. There will always be markets available if African farmers, either small holders or plantation owners, can efficiently produce quality exports of these crops. The second factor in the success of an export agricultural program is the availability of large sums of money, either private capital or government subsidies, which will enable the farmers to compete with their counterparts elsewhere in the world. In the case of the Sudan, Ivory Coast, and Kenya, there had already been great capital outlays to support the production of export crops long before these states had become independent. The economic infrastructure was in place and all the African governments had to do was to continue to develop that which it had inherited. It should be noted that whenever there is a healthy export agriculture, the governments and people, far from scorning continued European investment and open participation in the economy, have actively sought it. Thus there was no sharp break with the past; instead there has been a steady flow of outside capital into these states. This has been true even if the government is directly involved in managing the overall project such as in the case with the Gezira region of the Sudan.

The last and most obvious common feature of these three states is political stability. The Ivory Coast has had only one president, Felix Houphouët-Boigny, since independence and the majority of the people have been content under the one party system that operates there. Jomo Kenyatta, until his death in 1978, ruled Kenya for more than thirteen years as a benevolent despot, beloved by most and respected even by his political opponents. His successor, Daniel Arap moi, has continued the general policies laid down by Kenyatta. The governments of both the Ivory Coast and Kenya have been committed to a mixed capitalistic society since independence and welcomed foreign investment. The Sudan which has been politically the most unstable of the three has had a strong man government for more than a decade under President Jaafar al Niameiry. There was little fighting even in the disturbed decade after independence and the development plans for the extension of irrigated agriculture went on without serious modifications even during the periods of political instability.

The most obvious conclusion one can draw from this brief survey of agriculture is the central role it plays in the economy of every African state. Even those polities which are blessed with mineral resources will neglect the agricultural sector at their peril. In most African countries traditional approaches to agriculture are no longer sufficient to meet the challenges posed by increasing population. States formerly self-sufficient in foodstuffs are now being forced to import food at a time when more and more young men are leaving the farms for the allure of city life. Governments have been slow to recognize the crisis in traditional agriculture or pastoralism and in many cases have only begun to respond. In some states these responses have been piecemeal. Meanwhile, political instability, wars, and droughts have reduced formerly productive regions to wastelands. Confiscation of European property and subdivisions of estates for ideological reasons have also reduced the continent's ability to feed its people. Regions which at one time had a healthy export agriculture have, because of political interference, wars, or mismanagement all but destroyed this potential. President Julius Nyerere of

Tanzania may not have the specific solution, but he was certainly correct in his analysis of the problems not only for Tanzania, but for all of Africa. Given the spectacular increase in population in every African country, all governments must view the improvement of agriculture as having a priority as important as the limitation of population.

FIVE
Resources and Industrial Development

African traditional societies were designed for economic self-sufficiency. Whether pastoral or agricultural, the aim of the society was to provide enough food for its members. Any surplus could be traded to neighboring villages or clans for goods which could not be produced locally. Some of the markets became so important that they drew long-range traders who brought with them such desired items as salt or manufactured goods. The trans-Saharan trade brought to the savannah regions many important trade items from the Mediterranean regions which were exchanged for gold, ivory, or slaves. This same process was duplicated along the coastline of East Africa where the Zenj merchants traded finished goods for products valued in the Indian Ocean trade. To a lesser extent this pattern of long-range trade was duplicated westward from the middle Nile. Trade was a fundamental cause for the creation of such great kingdoms as Ghana, Mali, and Songhai in the west and the Monomotapa empire of the lower Zambezi region and a host of other smaller kingdoms which shared to some extent a centralized governmental system. The existence of centralized states in Africa and their dependence upon long-range trade tends to mask the economic reality underlying these polities. Trade in gold, ivory, pepper, salt, and manufactured goods was very important, but it never supplanted the village-based systems. The health of all the African empires rested upon the continued functioning of the agricultural and, in some cases, the pastoral sectors.

The economic linkage between the agricultural villages and the long-range traders was a system of barter. Trade goods were exchanged for raw materials using either the method of the dumb trade or more often by means of agents who were accepted in different societies. It is important to note that in very few places was there anything resembling a money system. This remained the case even after the arrival of European traders and the ascendency of the slave trade in coastal regions. Europeans tried very hard to introduce an inflated monetary system into the west coast trade but had to accept the demands of Africa rulers who controlled the trade. The slave trade was carried on throughout most of its long history by means of a modified barter system where the price of slaves and other services needed by Europeans was calculated in terms of goods. Even the acceptance in certain trade regions of wire or iron bars did not mean that the Africans had committed themselves fully to a monetary system.

The trans-Atlantic slave trade had profound effects upon portions of Africa. It aided in the centralization of government, the growth of African armies, endemic disorder, and the desire for certain items of trade which could be obtained only from Europeans. It should be noted that the direct effect of more than three centuries of slave trading was localized in the coastal reaches, mainly of West Africa. Rulers and traders in those areas zealously guarded the interior regions from the Europeans. It was not until well into the nineteenth century that European explorers braved the many dangers to explore the sources of the Niger, Nile, and Congo Rivers. Less than one hundred years ago most of Africa was still unexplored and most Africans had never seen a European. Their lives might have been changed slightly by being able to obtain such items as firearms from local or Arab merchants, but the direct economic effect of Europe was minimal. Then in a period of twenty years Africa was divided among the great powers and each then had to make good its occupation and establish a system of government for their areas. Only then were European economic systems introduced to most Africans. Familiarity with European economic practices throughout most of the continent is only a half-century old.

During the imperial period Africans were forced to conform to the European model in certain ways while being allowed to continue most of their old habits without penalty. Prices were established for goods, import and export taxes were established, and capitation and property taxes of various kinds were imposed. Gradually Africans altered their economic and social systems to conform to the new economic realities. Even such practices as bride price became transformed from payment in cattle to payment in currency. Barter still continued, but became increasingly less important and Africans in the twentieth century had to find ways of obtaining money.

Each European power imposed its own economic system and imperial presuppositions upon Africans under their control. The Portuguese and Belgians established economic as well as political autocracies. However, they had different goals. The Portuguese viewed their African territories in a neo-mercantilistic way where most of the economic benefits should accrue to the metropole. In the Congo after the lamentable early period under Leopold II, Belgium created a type of benevolent paternalism with a large portion of profits obtained being reinvested in the Congo. The ultimate goal of Belgian administration was to make the African into a European-type consumer and producer. The French and the British administered their areas with less clearly defined political or economic goals. However, in each empire economic as well as political power was firmly in the hands of the Europeans. Trading firms, banks, shipping companies, and mining ventures were all controlled by Europeans. Africans when associated with the government or private firms normally occupied low echelon positions. Fundamental decision making was normally reserved for a Board of Directors resident in either Paris or London. This autocratic situation continued to the eve of independence. Middle management positions remained out of the grasp of most Africans until the political climate had changed in the 1950s. Then there was a rush in most British and French territories to train Africans for higher level posts. Africanization programs had hardly begun when most African territories received their independence. In Belgian and Portuguese territories there were even fewer trained African managers than there were competent political leaders. Thus throughout Africa in a matter of a few months Africans who had been operating as low level employees in government and industry were suddenly propelled into the highest positions in the state, responsible for making the most crucial economic decisions.

Europeans had first become interested in Africa because of trade. This concern remained paramount throughout the imperial period. The French and British in the nineteenth century introduced such export crops as peanuts, cocoa, coffee, tea, and cotton to certain African areas. These crops along with timber, oil palm, and rubber remained the major concern of the governments of many of the colonies and private companies through the 1950s. The Belgians and Portuguese belatedly introduced some tropical crops in the twentieth century and continued to extract profits from their exports until forced to grant their colonies independence. Europeans controlled the trading companies which purchased and sold these exports and in some cases such as in Kenya, Rhodesia, and the Congo were responsible for producing the bulk of the export produce. In such areas the Africans were not only denied access to policy-making positions in trade, but also were discouraged from patterning themselves upon the Europeans who were so successful in cultivating such crops as tea, coffee, or sisal. Thus aside from the difficulties involved in converting land from traditional use to large-scale production, Africans were forced into a secondary competitive position with their European counterparts.

One motive for the European occupation of Africa had been the expectation of considerable profit from the mineral wealth of the unexploited areas. This hope was never fulfilled. Most African territories cost the imperial power more to administer than was gained in profits. There were exceptions. Copper in great amounts was discovered in northern Zambia and the Katanga (Shaba) region of the Congo (Zaire). Industrial diamonds were found in the Congo and in South-West Africa. Even in these cases full exploitation was postponed because of the depression. World War II and its insatiable demand for metals of all types caused the "Copper Belt" to boom and helped finance the exploration for new sources of crucial minerals. The period during and immediately after the war was one of discovery and the beginnings of exploitation of Africa's buried wealth. However, this period was also one of political ferment in Europe and the beginnings of devolution of power to the African elite. The realization of the potential in most mineral-rich areas of Africa coincided with the first experiments with African independence.

Africa's mineral wealth is not shared equally. Only a relatively few locales are blessed with a variety of minerals in quantity enough to make their exploitation profitable. Those states which do not have large mineral deposits must be considered separately from those which do. There are some African states where minerals are either nonexistent or exist in such small quantities that it is not profitable to extract them. Benin, Togo, Chad, Equatorial Guinea, Senegal, and Somalia are among the mineral-poor states. The major problem of such states is one of trying to provide the people the necessary services and reasonable development without having a large inflow of foreign capital. Such states encourage explorations for minerals with the hope that a major discovery will alter their poverty-stricken economies.

An example of such a metamorphosis is the discovery of iron ore in Mauritania. More recently Niger which once was a byword for a poor backward state whose government was kept afloat by French aid has been rescued by the finding of uranium in great quantities. It is estimated that Niger has the world's fifth largest reserve of this important mineral. French companies are just beginning to exploit the deposits and the government of Niger, no longer poor, can look with more optimism toward the future.

Of the sub-Saharan states, the Republic of South Africa which led the way with the discovery of diamonds and gold is the richest, having a variety of important minerals including chrome, manganese, asbestos, antimony, and uranium. South Africa is unique in Africa since it has a balanced economy, a large, well-trained managerial sector, an industrial base, and its own financing for the exploitation of its mineral wealth. Other mineral-rich areas such as Angola, Zimbabwe, Zambia, Zaire, and Gabon lack one or more of these factors which would give them independence of action. The early discovery of minerals in most African areas and the cost of development of that wealth was done by European or American firms. Some of these companies such as *Union Miniere du Haut Katanga* were firmly established in a monopolistic position before independence. Others were drawn to African areas because of the rumored presence of minerals in newly independent states and the expectation of great profits. No sub-Saharan African state with the exception of South Africa possessed the capital or the technical expertise in the 1960s to take advantage of its mineral resources. Yet the leaders of each of these states needed money in order to keep their governments afloat. Thus in the two decades after independence most African governments saw and took advantage of the benefits which would accrue to them as a result of cooperation with foreign firms.

Capital-poor Africa has benefited greatly from economic co-operation. Mauritania, once so poor that it could not afford its own capital city, obviously could not have expended the millions of dollars necessary to exploit the iron ore deposits discovered immediately before independence. Liberia, deeply divided between the up-country people and the dominant Americo-Liberians, first began to prosper after Firestone's considerable investments in rubber plantations during the 1920s. Then foreign capital flowed into the country in great quantities to move the high quality iron ore of the Bomi Hills to a newly built port. Gabon, which today has the highest per capita income of all

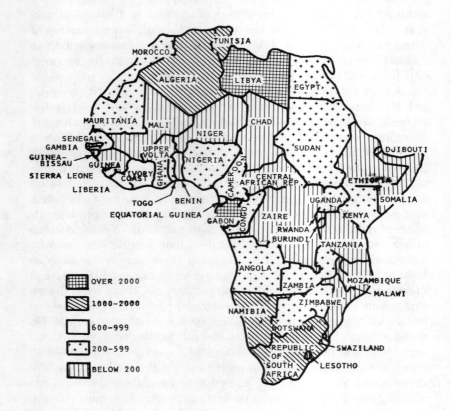

Per Capita Income

(in $)

African states, could never have taken advantage of its timber and mineral resources without French capital and expertise. The French are similarly involved in the development of Niger's uranium, the manganese of Upper Volta, and the diamonds and uranium of the Central African Republic. British, American, and South African capital was involved in the development of Zambia's copper industry and in the burgeoning mining industry of Zimbabwe, particularly of chrome, the one product in greatest demand in the Western world. In a similar fashion, Belgian companies and banks continued to support the many activities begun in Zaire before independence even during the five years of civil war after 1960.

Petroleum discoveries of the 1960s have been among the most important economic developments in Africa. Gabon, Angola, Ghana, and most recently the Cameroon have small amounts of petroleum, enough to counter the drastic economic blows rendered by the OPEC price increases of the 1970s. By far the most important oil discoveries were those made in Nigeria. Discovered first in the midwest and later eastern coastal zones, in the 1960s oil has brought the military and now civilian governments of Nigeria undreamed of wealth. Revenues from petroleum allowed Nigeria to crush secessionist Biafra in a three year war and then to reconstruct the war-shattered eastern areas. Nigerian petroleum is "sweet oil," low in sulphur and therefore in great demand on the world market. Even without the drastic increases in petroleum prices in the 1970s, Nigeria would have been wealthy by African standards. The average per-day production of petroleum in Nigeria over the past decade has been in excess of 2 million barrels. This has resulted in the influx of a huge amount of capital and the rapid development of Nigeria's port and transportation system and has enabled the government to launch broad and costly development programs which would have been beyond the conception of those political leaders who had led Nigeria to independence in 1960.

There are many benefits to a nation from the exploitation of its natural resources. Profits enable governments to sponsor improvements in all sectors of the economy, jobs are available which enable the workers to afford to purchase not only necessities, but desired luxury items such as automobiles, radios, and television sets. The demands of the extractive sector mean that more African technicians are needed and since most governments insist that their nationals be represented at all levels of management and development, there are positions created for African scientists, engineers, and managers. The trickle-down process does work, although in a minimal fashion, which means that even traditional Africans benefit although located far from the site of the mining, plantation, or forest areas which are the sources of wealth. In a further indirect fashion Africans benefit from the improved roads and communications system that the new wealth can purchase and their children have a better chance for education in an expanded school system.

There is a darker side to the economics of the fortunate states which have mineral resources to exploit. The first and most obvious factor is that all extractive wealth is finite. Once a ton of copper ore or barrel of oil has been removed, it can never be replaced. It may appear to African planners that their mineral wealth is relatively inexhaustable, but this is true of only a few items such as the bauxite of Guinea and the Gold Coast. Gold, iron, copper, manganese, and uranium mines will not continue to produce vast quantities forever. Petroleum, the black gold of the twentieth century, is particularly vulnerable. One has only to refer to the Spindletop oilfield of east Texas or Signal Hill in California, once major producers of petroleum in the 1920s, which are now almost totally exhausted. Thus it behooves the governments of states with petroleum reserves to control carefully the depletion of their major source of revenue.

A second factor, one which has more immediate significance, is that while African governments can control who will mine and under what conditions, they cannot control demand and hence are at the mercy of the developed world. There is a great similarity between the export of agricultural products such as coffee, cocoa, or peanuts, and extractive wealth. A shift in demand can drive the price of any of these products down to levels where it is hardly profitable to produce the goods or mine the minerals. Zambia and Zaire, for example, became victims in the 1970s of the continued fall in the price of copper. Over 95 percent of Zambia's yearly export earnings worth $1 billion comes from copper and zinc. The drop in the per ton price of copper, combined with ongoing transportation problems, has slowed Zambia's development to a standstill. In neighboring Zaire the devalued market for copper proved even more devastating. The shortfall in income finally exposed the faulty economic practices of the Mobutu government and complete economic collapse of this large, rich state was averted only by the indvidual actions of Western nations and the International Monetary Fund.

The stated objective of many African leaders soon after independence was to free their states from economic dependence upon the imperial power by moving rapidly toward industrialization. This has proved to be a dream as illusory as Pan-Africanism. Most African states are at least as dependent economically upon the non-African world as before independence. Industrialization if taken to mean heavy industry is still beyond the capacity of most African polities. Even where it is feasible such as in the refining processes from raw ore of copper and bauxite, it is more profitable to deal only with the first stages of refining and leave the later and more complex reduction to factories in Europe or the United States. The hopes of building an African iron and steel industry to utilize the high grade ore from Liberia or Mauritania has foundered on political differences between African states and on the reality of world competition. Industrialization is now generally defined in a less ambitious sense to mean the development of service industries and first stage reduction plants in the complex process of mineral and agricultural exploitation.

It is difficult to generalize about all of Africa and the development of the modern commercial and agricultural sectors since each state varies greatly from its neighbor. However, the gross distinction between rich and poor states is still helpful. The poorer areas have seen little investment either by foreign or local entrepreneurs. The bulk of industry in such states is normally located in the capital city or in areas close to the major producing areas. Most development is in service industries or in such agriculturally oriented endeavors as peanut decorticating, cotton ginning, and palm oil processing. In the major towns and cities small businesses have developed to service truck and auto transport, provide bread, beer, and general foodstuffs, and to sell and maintain a variety of Western goods. Certain factors such as the location of a major port and airline facility can mask the poorness of the overall economy of a specific area. Dakar, the most important port in French-speaking Africa, is certainly the best example of Western development which far exceeds what one would expect of an underdeveloped area such as Senegal. Tourism provided Kenya and Tanzania with much needed outside capital which had nothing to do with the development of the modern sector but rather exploited the wild animal resources of these states.

The richer nations in Africa have simply been able to develop more and better service industries and spread these into all urban areas of the country. Zaire, Zambia, Zimbabwe, Nigeria, and Guinea all possess mineral resources which are or have been in great demand in the more technically advanced world. The necessity of partially refining raw materials has resulted in building of new factories adjacent to the mining areas. In turn this has stimulated needed subordinate industries, particularly in construction. Cement, lumber, iron foundries, and truck and rail service facilities can be found in each of these states. Capital created by the mineral wealth in turn is invested in a wide variety of businesses designed to cater to the needs of suddenly affluent sectors of the society. In addition to those services found in poorer states, one will find milling and brewing companies, soft drink bottling works, auto and truck assembly plants, canning factories, and radio and television services. A Western visitor to Lagos, Lusaka, or Salisbury will be able to find almost all the small and medium businesses with which he would be familiar in a European city. States with agricultural as well as mineral wealth would also have plants directed at agro-businesses such as farm implement retail stores, fertilizer manufacturers, food preserving and canning facilities, textile plants, and cigarette factories. Zimbabwe with an economy balanced between mineral and agricultural resources and cut off from world trade for over a decade has probably gone farther in the direction of self-sufficiency than any other sub-Saharan state. Nigeria on the other hand is undoubtedly the richest of the new polities and because of its petroleum has attracted a far greater amount of Western capital than any other. Much of Nigeria's surplus capital, both government and private, has then been reinvested in a bewildering variety of service industries.

Cities with their promise of cash rewards have acted as lodestones, drawing young men from the country areas. Most of the migrants are disappointed, for not even the wealthiest African state can provide industrial employment for all those who wish jobs. Therefore the unemployment rate in all African areas is very high and these men without jobs pose a threat to the security of more affluent persons. Certainly they are one reason for the alarming rise in crime in all African cities. The unemployed also are reservoirs of resentment against whatever government is in power and therefore they can be utilized to help bring down offending regimes. The more celebrated coups in Ghana and Nigeria could not have succeeded without the covert support of the urban poor. Less well-known but even more to the point is the role played by the unemployed in the disturbances in the Sudan, the Congo, and the more recent violent overthrow of President William Tolbert's regime in Liberia.

Those more fortunate workers who do have jobs are also a continuing source of worry for those who operate the mines, ports, factories, and larger service industries. Since governments have been taking over more responsibility for the operation of the economic sector, they become directly involved in most labor disputes. Many African workers belong to labor unions which like their Western counterparts are pledged to improve the conditions of labor and increase the pay of their workers. The power and privileges of African labor unions vary considerably. In states with military governments the actions of any organization including labor unions must be measured against the probable repercussions. In other regions which allow more freedom the unions behave in ways similar to those in Europe or the United States. The decade of the 1970s was a period of economic disaster for many urban Africans. World-wide inflation fed by a series of major increases in the price of petroleum products cut deeply into the incomes of African workers. The increased costs of imports also made it difficult for governments to respond favorably to workers' demands for increased salaries. Thus there were a number of paralyzing specific and general strikes throughout the continent during the past decade. No state was spared labor disturbances, but some of the worst confrontations occurred in the Sudan, Senegal, and Nigeria. In the latter case a wide variety of strikes occurred despite the military regimes and the latent coercive power of the largest army in sub-Saharan Africa. Surprisingly the majority of the strikes were settled amicably with little loss of life. This was because the governments in most cases recognized the justice of the strikers' claims and moved quickly to mollify them with some concessions. Labor unions thus acted as a channel through which protests could be directed or specific economic wrongs within a society rectified. Dissatisfaction could be defused by the government or industry addressing itself to those specifics. When unions either were not strong enough to represent the urban worker or were afraid to act, the dissatisfaction became general and blended in with student and consumer complaints and could aid in unseating unpopular governments as in the case of Ghana or Liberia. Despite their recent generally pacific record, unions could become far more important in deciding the political destiny of a state. All that is needed is a continuation of unemployment and inflation combined with the intransigence of an unpopular government. One must keep in mind that the workers in Brazzaville were at the heart of the revolt that established the more doctrinaire leftist governments in the Congo or that Sekou Touré came to power in 1958 largely because of his control of the labor unions in Guinea.

Economic mismanagement of a nation's resources has many causes. Chief among them is the promotion of men to positions of great responsibility who have had no previous experience in managing complex systems. As already noted, all African states at the time of their independence were chronically short of educated or trained managers. The dominant political party in every new state had not only to organize a government but also to assume the management of a complex economy. Political pressures forced the leaders in the name of Africanization to dispense with European managers as quickly as possible and replace them with Africans. The mismanagement in any African state was usually not the fault of the upper and middle range managers of specific parts of the economy, but rested mainly with the government leaders. Many before independence viewed themselves as Marxists and almost all considered themselves to be socialists. Very few of the educated had any training in economics or business and therefore could not appreciate the devastating effect some of their policies might have upon the economy. Attempts to put into effect programs of nationalization, collectivization, and state-owned industries have had devastating results in many African states whose leaders were ideologues rather than pragmatists.

The best example of high-level mismanagement of a nation's wealth is still Ghana during the Nkrumah period. The British at independence left the new Ghanaian government a huge surplus which they had built up over forty years of closely managed budgets. Ghana's population was relatively homogeneous and the coastal and Ashanti regions were among the most developed areas in West Africa. The bulk of government revenue was generated by cocoa. The world market price for this crop was high and relatively stable during the first five years of Nkrumah's rule. Instead of establishing an evolutionary development plan for the nation, the new government attempted to achieve too much too fast. Ghana

Airways was formed and immediately entered into competition with long-established European airlines for routes in West Africa and to Europe. The Ghana government operated at the same time three different competitive large aircraft necessitating three different inventories of parts. Predictably the airline lost great sums of money. Many of the same mistakes in management were made in the operation of Ghana's steamship company, Black Star Lines. In order to construct the great dam over the Volta River at Akisombo, Nkrumah's government gave away far too much in concessions to the European and American companies who were interested in Ghana's aluminum resources.

Nkrumah also used Ghana's wealth to carry out his political dreams of a united Africa under his leadership. Loans were made to friendly states and expensive conferences were held, the last of which, the OAU meeting in 1965, was directly responsible for Nkrumah's overthrow. He had expended $50 million on preparing to host the meeting, hoping that this would give him a much needed triumph. Instead, the meeting was a defeat for Nkrumah's ideas. His one close advisor who understood economic realities, Komla Gbedemah, quarreled with Nkrumah over the unprofitable ventures undertaken by the state and was dismissed in 1963. Thereafter Nkrumah and his fellow ideologues went unchecked in their plans to create many state supported and operated industries. Most of these state corporations proved to be nothing but a drain upon the economy and some even forced their competitors in the private sector out of business. Corruption on all levels was rampant. Too many politicians and managers viewed their offices as a stepping stone to wealth. Even Nkrumah took note of this in his Dawn Broadcast when he called for the rulers to have only one car, one house, and one wife. Ghana was near banktruptcy before the fall in the world price of cocoa occurred in 1964. Western nations alienated by Nkrumah's previous hostile speeches and actions were reluctant to advance funds to stem Ghana's growing crisis. When money was loaned, it was generally on a short-term basis with high interest rates. An investigation team from the International Monetary Fund in 1965 was very critical of the state corporations and Ghana's dependence upon short-range inflationary loans and refused to advance funds until the government brought some order to its chaotic financial system.

Nkrumah's overthrow in February 1966 did not bring an end to Ghana's economic woes. A succession of governments during the next fifteen years struggled to ease the debt problem incurred during the glory years of Nkrumah. Two governments were over-thrown because of their economic policies. The first civilian government after Nkrumah, that of Kofi Busia, was soon sup-planted by the military because Busia wanted to impose harsh cutbacks at all levels in order to bring spending and income into line. His successor, General Acheampong, although renegotiating some of the loans, became a victim of the continued low price of cocoa and the increase in the price of petroleum products dictated by the OPEC countries. The successor military regime came to a violent end in mid-1979. Ghana once more with a civilian govern-ment was still an economic basket-case in 1980. The inflation rate stood at more than 100 percent, the urban unemployment rate was over 20 percent, there was a chronic shortage of staple items and spare parts, and strikes at all levels were endemic. The results of the type of leadership given by Nkrumah and his associates have proved to be long-lasting.

Another example of chronic mismanagement of an otherwise healthy state is Zaire. Born of Belgium's complete reversal of policy, the state was wracked by civil war within a few days of its independence in June 1960. Very soon the United Nations was caught in the morass of old hatreds and new political parties as it sought to end the fighting. For all its lofty stated objectives, the United Nations was not able to bring about a satisfactory peace settlement before it withdrew its peacekeeping troops in June 1964. Finally, Moise Tshombe, backed by some elements of the army and white mercenaries, forced an unquiet peace on the vast territory. The army leader, General Joseph Mobutu, soon seized power and has been able by controlling the army to maintain himself in power. He was able to do this largely because of the mineral wealth of Shaba Province. Even during the dark days of the civil war the mines kept operating and the supporting facili-ties were relatively untouched. Belgian technicians and managers stayed on during the fighting and Shaba was soon producing at the rate before the civil war.

In the years following his ascendency, Mobutu renegotiated all mining contracts to give the state mining companies a majority control of operations. The most important of these was Gecamines, the national copper mining company. Operations in Shaba became more closely attuned to the political realities of Zaire. The decade of the 1970s would have been difficult for Zaire even if its government had been efficient and there were no cor-ruption. The continued fall in the price of copper struck Zaire as hard as it did neighboring Zambia since two-thirds of the state's export exchange came from copper. Part of the shortfall was made up by Zaire's wealth in other minerals such as cobalt, gold, manganese, and zinc. The demand for Zaire's industrial diamonds was constant and it continued to be the world's largest supplier of these. Mobutu's foreign policy cost the state dearly. By backing his brother-in-law, Holden Roberto, in the struggle for power in Angola, he left Zaire open for reprisal attacks when Roberto's forces failed. Two different invasions of Shaba from Angola occurred in 1977 and 1978. Each of these was defeated but only with the aid of Moroccan, Belgian, and French troops flown in to bolster Mobutu's defeated army units. The second invasion left Kolwezi, one of the major industrial cities of Shaba, in a shambles. The invasion and subsequent harsh fighting interrupted mining operations throughout the mineral-rich region.

The size of the bureaucracy of Zaire increased many times over in the period after 1965. Many of these officials viewed their offices as sinecures requiring little in performance from them. Development plans of all kinds lagged behind their completion dates. The agricultural sector was damaged most since the civil wars had displaced hundreds of thousands of people and previously productive land was allowed to go back to the bush. The practice of paying officials for services which should have been given freely became the standard way of accomplishing anything. Corruption and inefficiency flourished on all levels. The rise in petroleum prices in the 1970s struck hard at Zaire's already precarious economy and Zaire was already drifting toward bankruptcy when the Shaba invasions began. By 1978 the inflation rate in the cities stood at 75 percent. This figure continued to rise until two years later it was estimated at 200 percent. Inflation combined with low wages and high unemployment meant that the people of Zaire, far from being able to buy luxuries, could not even afford the necessities. Once food-rich Zaire experienced food riots in some cities, notably Kinshasa in 1979.

President Mobutu possessed a hold over the developed world that Nkrumah never had. However much of an anti-imperialist, he has been a staunch anti-communist and Zaire contains too many minerals vital to the West to allow it to fall into total economic disorder. Therefore when Zaire's debts reached $36 billion and the government was defaulting upon $100 million per year, the Western nations acted. In June 1978 representatives of five states met and formulated economic rescue plans. These included the rescheduling of payments on outstanding loans and a cutback in overall expenditures with the goal of achieving a balanced budget. In 1979 the International Monetary Fund provided $150 million in standby credits. Western experts supervised the devaluation of the currency by 30 percent, the reorganization of the Central Bank, and controls over speculation, illegal transfers, and large loans to Mobutu's associates. Such radical economic changes dictated from outside may save Zaire from economic collapse, but they indicate how close this potentially wealthy state came to total bankruptcy because of mismanagement by its leaders.

The examples of Ghana and Zaire should not be taken as typical of all African states. They simply represent the best examples of what can happen when undue dependence upon outside capital is blended with economic naivety, ideological committments, corruption, and mismanagement. There is hardly a state in Africa which has not experienced to some extent the same elements which so devastated Ghana and Zaire. It is difficult for an outsider to know the depth of corruption in some African states. In East Africa the word *wabenzi* was coined to indicate the new class of economic and political managers who could be recognized by their possession of one or more Mercedes-Benz automobiles. Economic mismanagement was a major contributing factor in the military coups in Benin, Upper Volta, Chad, Togo, Nigeria, the Congo, Uganda, and Ethiopia. The most successful states in Africa are those which combined the possession of desired agricultural or mineral resources with a dependence upon Western management and a government which was relatively free of corruption, led by a strong man whose power to control the economy transcended his elective position. Jomo Kenyatta of Kenya and Felix Houphouët-Boigny of the Ivory Coast perhaps fit this model better than any other African leaders. Some of the smaller states such as the Gambia, Botswana, and Malawi, with few resources, have been politically stable largely because their leaders kept corruption to a minimum and forced the government to live within its means. They had been satisfied with modest economic gains and improved the well-being of most of the people while preserving the state from undue foreign pressure and major internal crises. The unsuccessful coup attempt in the Gambia in the summer of 1981 which cost the lives of hundreds of people showed that even such small states were not immune to the forces which have been so destructive in larger, more complex polities.

One must always be suspicious of announced plans for economic development in any African state. Much can happen between the pronouncement of economic goals and their finalization. Politicians, military governors, or economic amateurs can modify any development scheme out of all recognition. Nevertheless there seems to be a number of generally recognized problems common to most African states and many governments have announced programs designed to correct these. One of these common features is the belated recognition of the importance of agriculture in any scheme of development. For over a decade the agricultural sector in many African nations was given secondary priority to more grandiose schemes of economic improvement. However, with the growth of population and the abandonment of agriculture by so many young men, states such as Nigeria which were once self-sufficient in food now must import a significant quantity of the basic foods.

There are two differing approaches to increasing food production. One is socialistic where emphasis is placed upon nationalization and collectivization wherever possible. Guinea has quietly been following such an approach since 1958. The best known socialistic approach is that of Julius Nyerere and his *ujamaa* scheme. The other reaction to agricultural problems is the mixed approach where government attempts to correct the problems by giving direct aid and incentives to farmers to produce within a generalized free enterprise system. This is by far the most popular method. Its success in any given state depends upon the vision of the planners, the amount of capital to be expended, and the willingness of the farmers to cooperate.

Another set of problems common to most African states is the degree to which economic control is in the hands of foreigners. Even those political leaders who do not consider themselves socialists recognize the potential of neo-imperialism to undermine the political independence of their states. Ghana and Zaire have already been pointed to as examples of growing political instability because of dependence upon foreign investment, but the problem is endemic. By 1970 over 70 percent of all aid granted to African states was used simply to cover the costs of servicing earlier debts to foreign governments or private banks. Africans accuse Western firms and banks of retaining only a small percentage of the profits made either from manufacturing or the extractive industries in any African country. Instead of the bulk of profits being invested to develop the country where they had originated, they are utilized in the more highly developed West.

This feeling of being cheated has led many African governments either to nationalize entire industries or to assume controlling interest in key firms.

Banking has been a major target of African nationalists. At independence almost all banks in Africa were branches of European commercial establishments, a situation which in most states continued for over a decade. Key financial decisions were made by Europeans at times without reference to the goals established by the new governments. Soon the banks were being attacked for taking orders from European financial capitals and being the agents by which a country's profits were funnelled to outside agencies. Commercial banks also had established preferences for certain types of loans. They had a bias toward trade and commercial enterprise and were very dubious about financing improvements in the agricultural sector. For example, before Zambia created the National Commercial Bank, loans for agriculture amounted to only 4 percent of the money lent by banks. Practical reasons combined with national pride and a fear of neo-imperialism led first to the creation of state-supported banks and then in some cases for a state to nationalize all foreign banks.

Generally when the banks were nationalized it was as a part of a more general scheme. By the early 1970s most of the major extractive companies throughout Africa had been forced to accept the government as a senior partner controlling at least a 51 percent share. Generally nationalization proceeded slowly because of the danger involved in frightening those foreign agencies which had the investment capital so needed by African states. In some states only the extractive companies were affected; in others the financial institutions were also included. Where this has been the case there has been no appreciable slackening of European investment since there normally was enough profit to be made in a given industry that sharing with the government made little difference. Some states such as Nigeria, Zaire, and Zambia have proceeded to assume gradually direct control over much of the private sector. Zambia, for example, controls 51 percent of all the copper mines and banks, has nationalized all larger companies, and announced its intention of converting smaller businesses into cooperatives. Tanzania since Nyerere's Arusha Declaration in 1967 has systematically nationalized most of the means of production and launched operation *maduka* to replace private ownership of shops with state-owned cooperatives.

Despite the disasters of the Nkrumah years, Ghana has served as a model for other states in creating state corporations. The most successful of these state-sponsored companies have been those which purchased goods directly from the producer. Cocoa, oil seeds, timber, and coffee marketing boards have generally performed very well in the states which have them. The state assures a monopoly by making it a criminal offense for a private company to compete in purchase or sales of a specific commodity. The officials of a marketing board are appointed by the government. In the early years, especially in Ghana, this close linkage could spell disaster, but more recently a significant number of technocrats have been appointed and these experts make the boards run smoothly and with considerable efficiency. By cutting out the middle men in purchases, the marketing boards have been able to offer producers higher prices for their products. They have also been able to stabilize the internal markets by establishing beforehand the prices to be paid for a season's harvest. Despite the advantages, the boards are still prisoners of the supply-demand world market system. Although there has been some development toward cooperation between states in trying to maintain set prices for such items as coffee, the producing states, no matter what their internal organization, have not been able to dictate world market prices.

Closely related to state control of business or nationalization have been the attempts toward Africanization or as it is now called, indigenization. During the first years after independence, Africanization programs tended to concentrate on the work force. Pressure was brought to bear upon European-dominated companies to replace Europeans or Asians with Africans. Although this process resulted in some cases in lowered efficiency, it was generally successful in opening up a wide variety of opportunities in the private sector which had earlier been denied Africans. Most governments also replaced European workers as soon as possible. Some African leaders refused to be stampeded by pressures from job seekers and waited before replacing many of their European senior staff, thus assuring that Africans when assuming those posts would be better trained. Some governments, however, rushed to apply the spoils system and discharged competent Europeans in order to replace them with ill-trained Africans. By the decade of the 1970s, all African governments had dispensed with their European staffs except in some specialized areas.

Where there was a large number of Lebanese such as in Sierra
Leone and Nigeria, or Asians as in Kenya, Tanzania, or Uganda, it
was necessary for the governments to make laws reserving certain
jobs only for Africans. Uganda in a very short-sighted series of
maneuvers solved its overall Asian problem by deporting all of
them. The Kenyan and Tanzanian governments, recognizing what
an important role the Asians played in their economies, decided
upon evolutionary programs in order to assure Africans a chance
at positions then dominated by Asians.

Very soon most African governments recognized that
Africanization of the work force was not enough and moved to
restrict non-Africans in their control and operation of certain
businesses. The actions of the various governments giving preference to Africans involved in business were generally a part of
overall nationalization plans. The degree of interference and the
speed with which non-nationals were forced out depended upon
the state and the leaders' commitment to centralized control.
However, most states had by 1980 developed comprehensive
indigenization programs, even though many had not committed
themselves to total nationalization. The indigenization programs
differ from state to state, but most specify certain categories of
businesses which must be owned and operated by their nationals.
Thus Nigeria has twenty-two such categories and Ghana has nine-
teen. These include bakeries, garment manufacturing, taxi and
buses, and small retail businesses. There is generally a separate
schedule of larger businesses such as breweries, construction,
cement plants, petroleum distribution, and auto sales in which
nationals must have considerable interest. Nigeria has established
thirty-three such categories while Ghana has forty-six. In Ghana
their nationals' share of such business enterprises varies between
40 to 50 percent while in Nigeria the share is 40 percent. Most
other African indigenization programs are not as complex and
some such as Kenya exempt certain cities or specialized industries from the indigenization decrees.

There are good reasons for any African government to want to
control its own economy and seek to assure the well-being of the
people, and it is obvious that all governments have been pressured to be rid of the foreigners and reward citizens with their
jobs and businesses. There are severe dangers inherent in a doctrinaire approach to nationalization and indigenization. One of
the greatest is that such policies will frighten away the capital that
is so necessary to develop an embryo economy. Unless the

product to be obtained is a mineral in great demand such as uranium, diamonds, or petroleum, then capital will flow away from states which do not provide security for foreign investment or guarantees of reasonable profits. A second danger is the myth that Africans when placed in control of businesses will be less likely to exploit the people than would be the case with Europeans. In many African states indigenization did little more than transfer economic power from rich foreigners to rich Africans who had little concern for the plight of their fellow Africans. In Nigeria, for example, as far as selling is concerned, it has been estimated that only 0.1 percent of the population benefitted from the complex indigenization laws. The final problem of nationalization and indigenization has already been alluded to. Bureaucratic inefficiency and corruption have been rife in most African states. Nationalization can institutionalize and, therefore, protect these qualities. Ghana, Zaire, Nigeria, Uganda, and Tanzania have all had their economies seriously damaged by mismanagement and open corruption. Dedication, honesty, and efficiency are not qualities which can be established by the simple act of legislating for them.

Despite the differences, one point emerges with clarity. African governments by the mid-1970s had intruded themselves directly into every facet of the economy and those economies were firmly controlled by Africans. Thus despite differences in political and economic philosophy and fears of neo-imperialism, African governments have achieved control of their economic systems. Political leaders can no longer justify their poor performance in the economic field by pointing to the omnipresence of European or United States neo-imperialism. The pressures of the world market and in some cases of multinational corporations remain, but African governments have established over the past decade the mechanisms to control outside interference. Africans, within the parameters established by the world market, are themselves the governors of their own economies and the health of any state now depends largely upon the policies enforced by either military or civilian governments.

SIX
Political Stability

Without doubt those events in Africa most apparent to the casual viewer are the seeming unending series of coups and counter-coups, wars, and bloodlettings which at times verge upon genocide. Some of these events have a comic opera character such as the succession of Military takeovers in Benin and Sierra Leone in the 1960s or the posturings of Emperor Bokassa of the Central African Empire. What is not always understood is that behind even such ludicrous situations there exists very real tragedy, increased suffering, and loss of hopes by the African population. Although secondary to the long-range concern with population control, the search for political stability in each African state is the most pressing immediate problem. Without stability it is obvious that little can be done to address the host of other problems besetting African states.

Before analyzing in any detail the various kinds of African governments which have evolved in the past two decades, one should examine once again some of the reasons why those systems bequeathed by the European powers did not work as planned. First of all, no European power ever had a clear idea of its ultimate political responsibility toward its African territories. Acquired in haste, the political systems established were as direct as a given situation would warrant. Leaving aside the philosophical rhetoric of the first half of the twentieth century, one finds all African territories ruled in an autocratic fashion. Every important decision was made by a governor resident in Africa or by a colonial ministry at the metropole. If confronted by the question of types of responses sought for an independent African state, these officials would have laughed at the thought that independence would be granted sooner than fifty or one hundred years. They would have pointed to the illiteracy rate, the tribalism, and the great gap in training and education which separated the African from the European. Secure in the knowledge that there was time to develop Africans to European levels of political awareness, the government officials continued to rule in an autocratic and in many cases arbitrary manner.

The imperial world changed drastically after World War II. Empires were no longer the fashion. They were expensive to maintain and many subject peoples were prepared to force independence if necessary. Once again decisions as fundamental as those which launched the "scramble" seventy years before were made in London, Paris, and Brussels. However different the timing and method, each imperial power decided to give their African areas political independence while trying to retain economic control. It was obvious that European states with their quasi-democratic governments could not leave behind a series of autocratic African governments which would have been consonant with the type which had kept order during their more than half-century of rule. The ideal in the 1950s was to bequeath to the governments of independent Africa systems similar to the central government of the imperial power. This meant that in each state there should be some form of functioning representative government with elections open to as many people as possible. Such governments, of course, necessitated the formation of political parties and guarantees of freedom of speech, assembly, and the press. Losing political parties, like their European counterparts, could then become the loyal opposition while the winners recognized the rules of the game and would not take advantage of their newly won power. Thus in the decade of the 1950s the major European powers hastily prepared to depart from Africa, leaving behind as their chief legacy constitutions which enshrined the best principles of those liberal European governments which had been evolved over five centuries of trial and error.

In retrospect one wonders at the seeming naïveté of the parties involved in these high level transactions. European officials and businessmen were openly contemptuous of their African subordinates. Much of the bureaucratic maze constructed by Europeans in preindependence Africa had been designed to keep African corruption to a minimum. The upper echelon of the civil service was still staffed almost exclusively with Europeans. Africanization of the civil service had become a goal only after the war and in many places had just begun. There were few Africans in responsible positions in the police forces and the first Africans had been sent to European military schools in the early part of the decade. The weight of opinion of those Europeans who dealt most directly with Africans was that the quick devolution of power to

African political leaders was going to prove a terrible mistake. Many of these officers arrived at their conclusions not because they were racists or wanted to protect their own jobs. They pointed to the general illiteracy of the African population and the educational systems which were totally inadequate to provide the mass of Western-educated Africans needed to staff the government and business infrastructures of a new state.

No territory in Africa had a homogeneous population. Instead the population was divided into dozens, and in some cases as with Nigeria and the Congo, hundreds of differing clans, tribes, and nations. The leaders of these traditional societies had for reasons of convenience, economy, and in some cases philosophy, been supported by the Europeans while the Western-educated African before the 1950s had been scorned as a "white" African. There was, therefore, little sense of loyalty to the larger polities. This was reserved not for the state, but for one's own group. Antagonisms between "tribes" varied from suspicion to contempt to open hatred. Even among the Western educated there was little sense of that corporate responsibility which was the driving force behind European political systems. Rather, they looked first to their individual advancement and then to that of their immediate kinsmen, and finally to enriching their clan, tribe, or nation.

Despite the many reasons for a moderate, go-slow policy of political devolution, the European powers proceeded as quickly as possible to divest themselves of their imperial appendages. These had become not only economic liabilities, but their possession indicated that the European government was out of step with the liberalizing movements of the twentieth century. Some political parties in France and England had always been opposed to empire building, and the government of the United States, the banker for European recovery after the war, was implacably opposed to holding subject peoples against their will. The "winds of change" began to blow across the African continent and there were few European leaders in the late 1950s who would not bend to it. African political parties, once anathema to the Europeans, now became necessary and their formation was urged by the government. Men such as Houphouët-Boigny, Kwame Nkrumah, and Sekou Touré, once believed by European governments to be dangerous at best and traitorous at worst, were welcomed at high-level conferences where schemes for the rapid devolution of power to the small Western-educated minorities were enshrined in a bewildering number of constitutions.

There was one exception to the carefully planned transition from European imperialism to African constitutional democracy. This exception was Guinea which for a complex of reasons did not vote in 1958 to accept Charles de Gaulle's prepackaged plan for the Fifth Republic. It has been speculated that the leader of the *Parti Démocratique de Guinee* (PDG), Sekou Touré, a politician who owed his leading position to his association with labor unions, was probably pressured by the largest French union, the communist-dominated *Confédération Generale des Travailleurs* (CGT), to bring in a no vote in order to embarrass the Gaullists. For whatever reason, the reaction of the French government was swift. Guinea was declared to be outside the French Union, French officials and technicians were ordered home, and all equipment which could be moved was shipped from Conakry. Guinea was cast adrift with no cash reserves, forcing the officials of the PDG to put together a government overnight. These actions by France which obviously were designed to show other African territories what could happen if French wishes were flaunted had the direct opposite effect. Sekou Touré had announced his adherence to socialism, and his commitment to create a Marxist-oriented state found Western money markets closed to him. Prevented from getting the credits so desperately needed from the West, he turned to the Soviet bloc and to his fellow ideologue, Kwame Nkrumah of Ghana. From them he received enough financial help to survive the first year.

Guinea's inauspicious beginnings in retrospect may have been fortunate. It was not difficult for Touré and other party leaders to convince the people that the imperial powers were hostile. Building upon this fortress mentality, the entire nature of life in Guinea was slowly altered in the direction of a one-party socialist state. The political and economic structure which had emerged by the 1970s was not too different from the Chinese model. In recasting the state and society the PDG was blessed with a viable agricultural sector and huge commercially exploitable bauxite deposits. Touré, perhaps one of the most underrated African leaders, carefully orchestrated contracts and loans which enabled Guinea to receive capital for development from the cold war competitors—the United States, the Soviet bloc, and China. Guinea courted isolation from other African areas and for more than a decade carried on a propaganda war against the "neo-colonialists," particularly Senegal and the Ivory Coast. The army was disbanded and a peoples' militia, an extension of the party, replaced it. Centralization and collectivization have progressed further in Guinea than in any other part of the continent. In carrying out his programs, Touré has not hesitated to use force to drive out or imprison his political enemies and there have been a number of serious attempts upon his life. After more than twenty years of supreme power, Touré has managed not only to survive, but to mold the state and economy of Guinea into the image he desired. A pragmatist as well as a socialist, he made clear his independence of Russia by expelling all Russian diplomats and technicians in December 1961. Guinea, so different from much of Africa, shares with other states a concern about the future. Touré, the charismatic leader, is growing older. Have he and his party lieutenants been able to forge a political and social system that is not dependent upon the personality and skills of the leader, or will Guinea be forced to go through the destructive stages of growth so common elsewhere in Africa?

In other areas of sub-Saharan Africa, independent nations emerged as a result of a series of compromises between the Western-educated minority and the imperial government. In British-controlled areas this took the form of a series of constitutions for each territory. Thus within a decade Ghana and Nigeria, considered the most advanced of British African territories, each received three constitutions. Every successive constitution devolved more power and responsibility to African elective bodies and the executive responsible to the elected legislatures. Governors sensing the desires of their superiors in London acted as tutors to the future African heads of state, and some such as Sir Charles Arden-Clarke in Ghana shared authority with the designated African leaders long before it was suggested by the Colonial Office. When British authority departed from one of their dependencies, the former rulers could pride themselves upon the thoroughness of their constitution making which left behind variants of the Westminster model by which Britain itself was governed.

The French territories proceeded toward independence in a completely different way. However much the French-educated African might criticize the government of the metropole, he would have admitted that it gave him rights of participation in the political sphere and civil service equal to white Frenchmen. After World War II the rules for French citizenship were liberalized and largely elective councils in the territories and at the federation level replaced the nominated ones of the prewar era. More seats in the French National Assembly were assigned to African deputies. Thus Felix Houphouët-Boigny, considered in 1950 to be a dangerous radical, could become within five years a member of the Assembly and a subminister in the government of France. From this position he had great influence upon colonial legislation. The debates in the French government in the 1950s concerning Africa were devoted to finding some method of accommodating nationalist demands within the French empire. Few African leaders wanted anything more than a type of commonwealth system which would allow them to have all the economic advantages of being in the French empire and still gain positions of political power within their territories. The French Union, although still largely theoretical, was within practical reach when Sekou Touré of Guinea delivered his bombshell in 1958. Guinea's rejection of de Gaulle's proposal resulted in French overreaction and independence for the pariah. Within a short period other French African leaders, particularly Houphouët-Boigny of the Ivory Coast, Modibo Keita of the Sudan, and Fulbert Youlou of the Congo began to see the advantages of a political break with France. Within two years the French Union had been abandoned, the two great federations broken up, and most of the territories had asked for and received their independence. This *volte face* left behind African governments modeled roughly upon the institutions of government of the Fourth Republic with the executive headed by a Premier responsible to the legislature.

Preparation for independence was considerably less in the Belgian areas of present-day Zaire and the Trust Territories of Rwanda-Urundi. After World War I, the Belgians had established a paternalistic government which aimed at developing a Western type of economic life in these vast areas. Education was largely restricted to the elementary levels. Few Africans were given secondary schooling and no college education was available to them until 1954. As late as 1958 Belgian authorities believed that notwithstanding what was happening elsewhere in Africa, they could continue their policies which aimed at very gradual devolution of political authority to the Africans. Independence was seen as a distant goal at least a generation away. The independence of Ghana, Guinea, and the pending independence of the French Congo combined with small-scale political activity in Zaire itself convinced the Belgian government to abandon totally their long-range plans for political development and grant independence to their territories immediately. Within less than two years of that decision Zaire was declared independent and the Trust Territories soon afterward. The size and diversity of peoples of Zaire combined with almost complete political ignorance displayed by even the most sophisticated leaders spelled disaster. Within weeks of independence Zaire dissolved in civil war. Crisis succeeded crisis and for almost five years the country was wracked by warfare. Political affairs were stabilized only with the aid of the United Nations and the emergence of the military. Less well-known were the disorders in Rwanda and Burundi which led to the deaths of hundreds of thousands of Bahutu and Watutsi in the decade after independence. Belgium's hurried attempts to provide democratic government structures for its territories after decades of paternalism are perhaps the most searching indictment of European imperialism in Africa.

No African state retained for very long the system of government established at independence. The most general alteration was the conversion of the systems of responsible governments into republics. Although there were many differing reasons for this change, two seem to be most common. African leaders by changing to a republic could in a minor way declare their further independence from the imperial power. Even more important, a republic allowed for the separation of executive power from the legislature. The head of a party could become President, a position unchallenged in the executive sphere. He could then use his prestige and authority as President to undermine any other competitive power center in the state. Patronage alone gave him many opportunities to wean away adherents to any other political party. As chief executive he could manipulate a ministry whose members owed allegience only to him. Through them he directly controlled the police and the armed forces. Very soon in most independent African states the party leader became more important than the party itself.

The ruling party in most African states even before separating executive from legislative power moved quickly to end all open opposition to the newly created government. This was done in a number of ways. The least objectionable was to use patronage to dislodge key members of the opposition from their parties. In Kenya the once powerful Kenya African Democratic Union (KADU) had by the skillful actions of President Kenyatta been reduced to only a small ineffectual legislative group within two years of independence. Much the same process could be observed in Ghana, Zambia, the Congo (Brazzaville), and the Gambia. The media became a major weapon to discredit the opposition. Newspapers attacked those who opposed government policy as disloyal. The idea so firmly entrenched in Western states of the loyal opposition was never given an opportunity to develop in most African states. Rather, they followed the lead of Kwame Nkrumah of Ghana who claimed that the manifold problems of independence demanded the full effort of the nation guided by the ruling party. To criticize policies and programs, therefore, was not evidence of only a difference of opinion, but was dangerous, a threat to the ultimate future of the state. It was only a step beyond to enshrine this idea into law, making the ruling party the only recognized organ of political activity and banning all opposition parties. By the mid-1960s most African states were one-party states and in most, all criticism of the government, the leader, or the party was dangerous. Opposition was thus driven underground.

In the first years of independence the central government in most states moved to extend its direct control over the entire country. In French and British territories the traditional chief and councils had played an important role in local government before independence. The new governments of the Westernized elite under the guise of the need for modernization moved quickly to reorganize local governments. This was usually done by redistricting the country and giving the new central government control over the traditional authority or at least shared power with them. The chiefs were thus rendered impotent in practical politics, being retained only for ceremonial purposes. This modernization went further in states such as Ghana, Sierra Leone, Zambia, and the Ivory Coast where the traditional authorities posed a potential threat to the autocracy of the one party. In Kenya, Tanzania, and elsewhere where traditional power was already diffuse, the need for stringent central government action was less. However, the task was accomplished and the primary authority in the traditional sectors had been assumed by the central government in all African states within a decade of independence.

Many African polities, once the level of a one-party central state had been reached, became relatively stable. Economic and political change in such regions proceeded slowly and deliberately, controlled by a strong man in his dual role of party chief and head of state. Economic wealth was a supporting factor in the continuing stability of these states, but was certainly not the key factor. The most important reason appears to be the strength of the party leader and the way he transmitted his vision of the future into viable actions which could win the support of all segments of the population. This does not mean that in such states there has not been corruption, inefficiency, and political crises. However, these were never allowed to escalate to the level where the masses of people lost confidence in the government or associated the leaders directly with any of the problems which arose. The listing of political leaders of states which fall into this category is a roster of the most distinguished African statesmen: Jomo Kenyatta of Kenya, Kenneth Kaunda of Zambia, Hastings Banda of Malawi, Felix Houphouët-Boigny of the Ivory Coast, Léopold Senghor of Senegal, Ahmadou Ahidjo of the Cameroon, and Omar Bongo of Gabon all maintained undiminished authority and popularity after independence. Personal freedom as well as the ability to criticize the government has been abridged in all these states, but the positive aspects of the one-party rule has overridden any dissatisfaction caused by restrictions upon individual freedom.

Other states encountered a variety of problems which were beyond the capacity of the civil government to solve. These polities could be called complex immature national entities. Many of these such as Nigeria or Zaire were only geographic expressions at the beginning of their independent existence. Composed of hundreds of differing peoples, loyalty was not given to the central authority figure who was viewed by a majority not as the leader of the country but as a representative of only one fraction. Zaire's problems surfaced immediately after independence and order was restored only after a blood bath which lasted for half a decade. At one time there were at least half-dozen competitive governments operating in the former Belgian possession. The state was saved only by military action of the central government which counted upon United Nations support and the use of mercenary soldiers. Zaire's government by 1965 had scarcely any resemblance to the complex political entity planned for by the Belgians five years before. President Mobutu has controlled Zaire for the past fifteen years not so much because he maintains the fiction of a civilian regime, but because he has been able to retain control of the army and police. The twin invasions of Shaba Province from Angola in March 1977 and May 1978 directed by his political enemies showed how precarious is his government.

He was in danger of losing his domination of the army and was saved only by the intervention of Belgian, French, and Moroccan forces.

Nigeria was more complex than Zaire. At first observers tended to minimize the divisive factors since Nigeria was a federation of four regions. Each had an important role to play in decision making and each was controlled by a different political party which represented one of the major groups of people. The northern government was dominated by the Hausa-Fulani, the Mid-west by the Edo speakers, the West by the Yoruba, and the East by the Ibo. Cultural and political differences between Nigeria's people and the religious split between Islam, Christianity, and animism far from being reconciled by the divided nature of government were actually exacerbated by it. The in-fighting between the political parties, the patent selfishness of many of the leaders, and the inefficiency of government agencies were all made worse by the rampant corruption which touched every level of government. One crisis followed another—the suspension of civilian government in the West, the treason trial of the leaders of the Action Group, the census of 1963, and finally the elections for the Western regional legislature. With each confrontation between parties, the general support of the population for their elected representatives eroded further. Venial politicians and corruption, combined with restrictions rather than expansion of freedom and opportunity, had converted the public into enemies of the politicians and the institutions they represented. Thus when the bloody work of the first military coup of January 1966 was finished, there were few who lamented the passing of the civilian government so painstakingly created by British and Nigerian constitution makers only a few years previously. In the immediate aftermath of the coup, the dead politicians had few mourners even in the North, the homeland of the Sarduana of Sokoto and Prime Minister Balewa. Nigeria awoke to a military government which would remain until 1980. During this long period there would be three coup attempts, two of them successful, and the bloodiest civil war in the modern history of Africa.

Uganda provides a further example of the fundamental weakness of a British-designed liberal constitution. The only strong allegiances in Uganda were local and these had been encouraged during most of the seventy years of imperial rule. The promises, direct and implied, made to the Baganda people were ignored in the desire to prevent the breakup of Uganda into discrete kingdoms. The Kabaka was exiled and police power used to bring Buganda into a federal state with all the trappings of responsible government and the sacrosanct concept of one man—one vote. From the beginning the government of Prime Minister Obote was plagued not only by the normal opposition elements, but also by the deep-seated detestation of the Baganda for a system of government which they did not want. Obote used the typical means of patronage and pressure to render his political enemies harmless but these did not work in Buganda and eventually he sent in the army, deposed the Kabaka, and thus assumed the direct rule of that reluctant kingdom. Other elements such as inexperience, inefficiency, and corruption aided in bringing down the civilian government of Uganda. However, the most important reason for Obote's overthrow by the military in January 1971 was his inability to reconcile the traditional elements, particularly those in Buganda, to his regime. For this the independence constitution was largely responsible.

These examples of Zaire, Nigeria, and Uganda are only the most glaring of the many cases where the civilian governments, acting within the context of logical, Western-style constitutions, were not able to meet the needs of the people. Benin, Sierra Leone, Rwanda, Burundi, Upper Volta, the Central African Republic, Chad, and Liberia all fit into this category of states whose liberal governments failed and were supplanted by the military whose leaders promised an end to corruption and the establishment of economic policies which would end inflation and bring a variety of direct benefits to the ordinary citizen.

There is another category of reality which negated the best intentions of the constitution makers. This concerns the vast cultural and historical differences between the Muslim and non-Muslim population in a given state. The boundaries of every nation in the Sudanic zone previously controlled by France and Britain were drawn with no concern for the indigenous populations. Thus in addition to tribal and clan differences there was a division in most states between the Muslim groups in the north and the animists and Christians in the south. This division was reinforced by an ethnic division. The majority of northern Muslims were Berber or kindred pastoral people while the dominant Christians of the south were black. Western-style education and training before independence, however slight, had been a near monopoly of the non-Muslim populations. Very little attention had been given by French administrators in preindependence negotiations to the small nomadic populations of the north in their French West African Federation. The result was that all these areas were dominated during the immediate postindependence period by black Christian politicians who concerned themselves mainly with maintaining the support of the tribal populations of the south. The problem outlined above, although most noticeable in the Sudanic area, also applied to the West African countries of Upper Volta, Togo, and Benin, and was a major factor in the continuing political instability of those states.

Although the division between Muslim and non-Muslim was a factor in the politics of Senegal, Mali, Niger, and Nigeria, it was particularly crucial in two states. As a part of the agreement by which Sudan received its independence on January 1, 1956, three southern provinces were turned over to the Muslim-dominated government in Khartoum. This was done despite the fact that the south had previously been administered as an adjunct to Uganda. The population of the southern Sudan was either Nilotic or Bantu animists harboring a deep-seated dislike of northern Muslims who had raided and pillaged the south for slaves in the nineteenth century. Southern leaders were generally Christian and did not look forward to continued domination by officials appointed from the distant capital. Hostility between the two sections resulted in violence as early as 1956. As more villages became involved, the government sent ever larger military contingents to the south and the violence escalated. At one time almost 20,000 Sudanese regular trops were operating against the southern guerrilla force, the *Anya Nya*. Despite the expenditure of millions of dollars and thousands of lives, the civil war dragged on and was one of the reasons why the Sudan had five different governments before the military coup of 1968 brought Jaafar Muhammad al Niameiry to power. He, in turn, survived a number of abortive coups and finally brought an end to the long conflict in February 1972. Al Niameiry recognized the right of the south to have its own legislature and executive empowered to act in all areas except defense, currency, and foreign affairs. This federal system allowing for maximum southern self-determination not only has brought peace to the south but has enabled al Niameiry to consolidate his control of the central government and to embark upon a series of important development plans which would have been difficult, if not impossible, to achieve had the war continued.

Another Sudanic state whose difficulties can be traced to the inadequacy of the independence constitution in recognizing the

Muslim minority is Chad. Chad in contrast to the Sudan had political power concentrated in the south where the black, French-educated political leaders lived. The wandering Muslim groups of the northern desert lands were largely ignored. By 1965 there had developed well-organized schismatic movements in northern and eastern Chad. A portion of Chad's army in Tibesti mutinied in 1968 and joined the rebels who by this time had the active support of Muammar Qaddafi, the quixotic ruler of oil-rich Libya which borders Chad in the north. Unable to contain the revolt, President Francois Tombalbaye invoked Chad's defense treaty with France which responded by despatching troops including elements of the Foreign Legion to the troubled regions. Despite such aid, the northern areas by 1970 were almost beyond control of the government. President Tombalbaye then made a major tactical error in trying to impose upon the nation certain cultural practices of his own tribe. In response, Chad's military in April 1975 seized power, killed the president, and created an autocratic regime under the control of General Felix Malloum. However, he could not conclude the civil war, and by the end of 1978, the rebels controlled most of the countryside. Malloum tried a coalition government which failed; he was deposed and after serious fighting in the capital fled the country in February 1979. After that date the insurgents attempted to create a stable government but all floundered because of the personal ambitions of different leaders. Each of the protagonists had their own private armies and each attempted coalition failed despite mediation attempts by the Organization of African Unity, France, and Nigeria. The already weak economy of Chad was all but destroyed during the fighting and the major city and capital, N'Djamena, was in rubble by the time Qaddafi dispatched troops, tanks, and aircraft in 1980 to support one fraction headed by Goukouni Oueddei. Order of a type has been restored by the armed intervention of an outside state and may possibly be maintained because of the threat of further Libyan interference and the exhaustion of Oueddei's enemies.

These brief glimpses at a few of the disturbances which made a mockery of the liberal constitutions of the postwar period indicate one thing very clearly. In order to govern an African state with a modicum of success the ruler must be in firm control of all agencies of coercion in the state. In a minority of instances leaders have been able to accomplish this through a civilian government created by the legal actions of either the people or constituent assemblies. Thus in Kenya, Botswana, Zambia, the Ivory Coast, and Malawi, the army or police have remained servants of the elected government and amenable to control by the civilian head of state. In other instances such as Guinea and Tanzania, the army as such has been disbanded to be replaced by a type of people's militia which is an adjunct to the ruling party and designed to further its ideology. So far this system has been successful in keeping the raw power of an armed force diffused and allowing the party leaders to use the militia in any way they decide. By far the most typical type of secure government in Africa has been a military form where the officers commanding obedience from their subordinates turned out the civilian rulers, arrogated power to themselves, and continued to maintain whatever regime they wished by the threat of the military.

The African military in all recently independent states was a curious amalgam of professionalism and untried, unproven soldiers, many of whom had only the most rudimentary educations. Before independence the military units conformed to the patterns of the imperial power in terms of training, discipline, and equipment. Beginning in the early 1950s there was a concerted drive in France and Britain to train African officers to assume the role then assigned to Europeans in the African forces. These men thoroughly imbibed the military traditions of the metropole. A few of the better officers had advanced to company level command by the time their country became independent. Advancement was rapid in the first few years following independence as the European senior officers were phased out and their places taken by Africans. Thus a captain would be advanced within three or four years to the rank of lieutenant-colonel or in some cases colonel. Despite the excellence of some of these men, they were handicapped by not having the experience of gradually escalating responsibilities. In some cases the military tasks assigned them were simply beyond their capacities. Nevertheless, during the early days of independence most officers trained in the European concepts of a nonpolitical army strove to maintain their neutrality in the face of the declining effectiveness of the civilian regime. Only when it became obvious to some that conditions in the state would not improve did they begin to think of acting against the constituted authorities. In a few cases they were spurred to such action by cuts in the military budget, low·pay, the drying up of quick promotions, and the fear, as in the case of Ghana, that the army might be replaced by some type of militia.

Some observers of Africa in the early 1960s discounted Africa's military as an effective political force since most of the armies were quite small. Such conclusions rested upon abstractions from the European experience where any military takeover would be in opposition to the views of large segments of the population who were schooled in the sanctity of civilian government. In such nontypical European countries as Spain and Italy in the 1920s, it had been necessary for the army to be large enough to overawe the population. However, as events developed in Africa, the size of the military force involved was always a secondary consideration. By the time the military staged its rebellion the civilian regime in most African states had normally proved its corruption and incompetence. The mass of people, at best apathetic to events which did not directly concern them, had no intention of rising up against the military to protect already discredited regimes. Those Europeans and American political scientists who had discounted the military had obviously forgotten how coercive a tank and a few men with machine guns could be when facing an unarmed population.

A portent of the power of the military came with the overthrow of Sylvanus Olympio, the brilliant, economically conservative president of Togo. He had viewed Togo's small army as a luxury which a poor state could not afford and planned to cut its size. There were many Togolese ex-service men who, on the contrary, demanded that the army be enlarged in order to reenlist them. The debate between Olympio and his army leaders was ended in January 1963 when the military seized the capital city after killing the president. Those who planned the coup had no specific program in mind other than the army issue and quickly turned the government over to civilian control. The precedent, however, had been set. When the civilian government once again could not meet the army's expectations, it was set aside in 1967 by another coup led by Colonel Etienne Eyadema. Although promising a quick return to constitutional government, he and the army have shown little sign of implementing his promise and the military is still fully in control of the small, heterogeneous state.

Another early example of the power of the military was the Sudan where the army commander, General Ibrahim Abboud, intervened in the internecine struggles between various political factions in November 1958. The military regime he and the Supreme Military Council imposed on the Sudan illustrates very clearly some of the major limitations upon army rule. The problems attendant upon a generally depressed economy which had only one major product to export could not be solved by simply giving orders. The devastating civil war in the southern Sudan continued as did political factionalism. It was also apparent that military training did not automatically make a person competent to carry out the complex tasks of government. Dissatisfaction which had helped bring Abboud to power continued and finally rioting students and government employees brought down his government in October 1964. Instability continued and another military coup, that of Colonel al Niameiry, occurred in 1968. His regime had to survive three major uprisings and he overhauled the system of government twice within the next five years. The government of the Sudan has since been stabilized not only because of al Niameiry's firmness and the loyalty of the armed forces, but because of improved economic conditions and the forging of closer political links with Egypt and most of the oil-rich Islamic states of the Middle East.

The most celebrated of all African military coups was that which in early 1966 toppled Kwame Nkrumah from power in Ghana. In many ways the first Ghana coup provided a high standard of behavior seldom seen later. The military units were led by young, idealistic, capable officers, Colonels E. K. Kotoka and H. R. Ocran and Major A. A. Afrifa. The fear that Nkrumah planned to do away with the military could be considered a self-seeking reason for rebellion. However, this reason blended in with the generalized concern over Nkrumah's mismanagement of the country and the realization that only the military had the power to bring down his regime. After the coup was successful the Ghanaian military promised an early return to democratic procedures and civilian control. The military government of Ghana headed first by General Ankrah and later by Afrifa struggled to bring some order to the economy and to renegotiate the killing burden of debts contracted by Nkrumah. They began to phase in some democratic procedures; the officers retired after the adoption of a new constitution guaranteeing civilian control and the election of Kofi Busia as President in October 1969.

The Busia government discovered that implementation of conservative economic procedures in order to deal with the economic crisis was very unpopular. Attempts to cut expenditures alienated a new group of the military and the second civilian government of Ghana was overthrown in January 1972 by forces loyal to Colonel Ignatius Acheampong. The long tenure of

Acheampong and his military and civilian advisors illustrates once again that the military does not possess a magic formula for solving a nation's problems. They merely possess the weapons with which to overawe the public. Any chance that Acheampong would succeed where his predecessors had failed was negated by the series of extreme price rises in petroleum dictated by the OPEC states in the mid-1970s. These triggered world-wide inflation which combined with problems with cocoa meant that Ghana in 1978 was in worse economic condition than when Acheampong seized power. Acheampong's popularity declined drastically over the years, particularly because of his negative attitude toward a return coup, Acheampong was supplanted by another officer, General Sam Akuffo, who set in motion the mechanisms for a quick transference of power from the military to civilian control. Before this could be accomplished a revolt of junior officers and noncommissioned officers led by Flight Lieutenant Rawlings occurred in May 1979. These young plotters reflected the attitudes of the mass of urban Ghanaians who wanted to punish those responsible for the apparent waste and corruption at all levels of the government. Self-constituted military courts rounded up hundreds of former officials. They were tried, sentenced, and many given long prison terms. Some of the most important military and civlian officials including Afrifa, Acheampong, and Akuffo were executed. After the bloodletting, elections for a new government took place, Lieutenant Rawlings returned to military duty, and President Hilla Limann's party came to control a third civilian government of Ghana. However, the problems which triggered the previous military takeovers still remain and the armed forces could at any time reimpose their control over the troubled state so shamefully governed by Nkrumah.

Nigeria in this same period was undergoing a similar but ultimately bloodier set of disturbances following a January 1966 coup. The government established by General Ironsi was overthrown in July and Ironsi was executed. His fellow officers in the Federal Military Government chose Colonel Yakuba Gowon to replace Ironsi just before the killings of the Ibo in the north by Hausa and Faulani fanatics set Nigeria on the road to civil war. The secession of the eastern region which took the name Biafra led to a thirty-month war which proved very costly in both money and human life and suffering. Nigeria's military government paid for the war and later the reconstruction efforts with its ever increasing petroleum revenues. By the mid-1970s Nigeria was the world's fifth largest producer of petroleum, and the government had more money than most Nigerians had ever previously imagined. Charges of mismanagement, corruption, and lethargy against the Gowon government had become widespread when his colleagues took advantage of his absence from Nigeria in July 1975 to stage a relatively bloodless coup and replaced him with General Murtala Mohammad. Where Gowon had been cool to suggestions of bringing back civilian rule within a reasonable time, Murtala gave a definite date for this transference, promised to abolish corruption, and to see that the wealth of Nigeria was more equitably distributed. He did not live to carry out his promises because he was assassinated by some of his fellow officers in an abortive coup. General Olusegun Obasanjo who succeeded him as head of the military government carried out the complex devolution of authority. Political parties were formed and general elections held for state legislatures and executives, a federal legislature, and for an executive president. In October 1979 Obasanjo turned over authority to the newly elected president, Shehu Shagari, and Nigeria's government returned to civilian control for the first time in more than thirteen years. Like Ghana, the problems of unemployment, inflation, and clan and tribal hostility still remain. It is not far-fetched to believe that if Shagari is not able to control these centrifugal forces, then the leaders of Africa's largest army would not hesitate to interpose themselves once again and return the state to military autocracy.

This extended discussion of the problems of Ghana and Nigeria could be duplicated in some measure for every state in Africa which has had a military government. There are always problems unique to a specific state, but the primary ones seem to be common to all nations which have seen the military assume control. Therefore, without giving precise details of the situations in Uganda, Ethiopia, Sierra Leone, Liberia, and the other African states which have or have had military regimes, certain conclusions can be drawn about power, freedom, and stability throughout the continent.

It should be obvious to all observers that political democracy of the Western European variety has failed in Africa. Most African societies had never practiced anything remotely similar. One of the sacred precepts of modern democratic societies, that of one man—one vote, was completely foreign to a majority of Africans in any state. During the sixty year imperial interlude, the Euro-

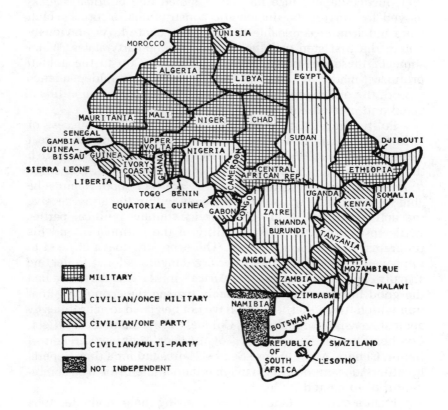

MILITARY

CIVILIAN/ONCE MILITARY

CIVILIAN/ONE PARTY

CIVILIAN/MULTI-PARTY

NOT INDEPENDENT

**Political Map Showing
Types of Governments**

pean powers ruled by means of specialized autocracies. Only in the brief period before independence was there any attention paid to preparing the people and their leaders for the peculiar responsibilities of democratic government. One should not be surprised that once independence had been gained, the political leaders moved to convert the democratic constitutions to forms which were much more amenable to their own control. As previously noted, the first step was the creation of one-party states. When some of these one-party states failed to live up to the golden promises made by political leaders in the preindependence period, the only agency with countervailing power, the military, acted and created another type of authoritarian state.

Politics in Africa is personality oriented. Thus success or failure of military as well as civilian regimes depends to a great extent upon the leader. If he possesses all those qualities by which the Ethiopians define a *tillak sew*, a strong man, then his chances of imposing his will upon the country are very good. He must be able to control the schismatic elements within the army, receive the active support of the civil service, outlaw political parties while restraining the overt hostility of the politicians, and his programs must appear to work. The economy does not need to improve to any extent, but it is very dangerous for it to decline sharply. The most successful of Africa's military leaders have had the good fortune not to appreciably worsen the economic situation which they inherited, and have not hesitated to act ruthlessly against any signs of disloyalty. Colonel Seyni Kounteche of Niger, Colonel Etienne Eyadema of Togo, Major Mathieu Kerekou of Benin, General Mobutu Sese Seko of Zaire, and for a time General Ignatius Acheampong of Ghana maintained their rule by a combination of force and guile.

Even a cursory glance at events during the period after 1965 indicates how chronically unstable much of Africa has been. Only a few states have been able to avoid coups and military authoritarians. In some cases such as Sierra Leone, Benin, Ghana, and Nigeria, the existence of army rule did not itself guarantee stability as one segment of the military challenged the group which controlled the state. In many other places such as Zaire and Mali, the military leaders after enjoying a period of power exchanged their uniforms for civilian garb while still dominating the new civil governments. In only a few states did the military leaders totally lose contact with reality and abandon all attempts to improve the lot of the people. Such were the tragic cases of Idi Amin in Uganda, General Jean Bokassa of the Central African Republic, and the competitive leaders of the private armies in Chad. A series of miracles would be needed to repair the damages done to the economy and peoples of Chad and Uganda. The sufferings and unnecessary deaths of millions of Africans in these two areas as well as in Zaire, Nigeria, Rwanda, Burundi, Ethiopia, and Somalia, although largely ignored by the outside world, can never be fully justified by those who would ascribe these events merely to growing pains.

The Republic of South Africa, Zimbabwe, and the ex-Portuguese territories are special cases. The former because of the presence of millions of whites who control economic and political power and who have sanctioned a political regime which denies equal access to that power by either the Colored population or the majority Bantu. The Republic is a curious combination of a fully representative government for whites based upon democratic principles and an authoritarian regime geared to the repression of blacks. Despite press reports, South Africa has not witnessed major confrontations between the races in the past two decades. Neither have there been any genocidical purges and it is probable that the white officials are correct when they claim that the Bantu in South Africa are in much better condition economically and have as much freedom as they would under the military and one-party regimes north of the Limpopo. However, the potential for violence is so much greater in South Africa than elsewhere in Africa because the increasing demands of blacks for an end to apartheid could lead to the mass of Colored and Bantu rising in revolt against a superbly armed and dedicated white minority. Such an eventuality conjures up the specter for the future of a massive blood bath. Until some compromise between the legitimate demands of nonwhites and the goals of the more advanced white community can be made, there will be the constant threat of violence in this, the most advanced state in Africa.

For differing reasons Zimbabwe, Angola, and Mozambique continue to be politically volatile despite the success of African liberation movements in defeating the dominant white power structures in these states. Mozambique has questionable stability because of its strategic location and the positive indication that the radical socialist program espoused by the FRELIMO government has been a failure. Economic distress very often breeds opposition and it is not clear at this time that Samora Machel could survive a serious challenge to his position. Angola continues to be unstable half a decade after its independence from Portugal. Despite military aid from the Soviet Union and the presence of a large Cuban force, it is not certain that President Dos Santos is fully in control of his government. Some observers claim that he is a pawn of those who placed his party in power and that the most fundamental decisions are made by the Soviets. The civil war in the south continues as Jonas Savimbi and his guerrillas firmly based in Ovimbundu territory refuse to recognize the Luanda government as legitimate. There is no indication that he is prepared to compromise and that Dos Santos has enough strength to defeat him. The political situation in Angola is made worse by the possible alignment of the cold war opponents on opposite sides with the Western powers choosing to funnel massive amounts of aid to Savimbi. Zimbabwe remains a region of potential trouble, not only because of the continued presence of a highly educated and trained white minority which only recently surrendered power to the Bantu. Just as in Angola, there was a split in the guerrilla forces which gained the final victory over the whites. The head of state, Robert Mugabe, with his power base in Shona country, has had to deal with the open challenge of his erstwhile political ally, Joshua Nkomo, whose followers are the Ndebele of the southwest. So far there have only been a few cases of armed clashes between the two groups, but the personal ambitions of various politicians and the historic antipathy between Shona and Ndebele could cause serious trouble.

In conclusion of this all too brief survey, what should be said of the politics of Africa? First, the general failure of European-style constitutional government should be restated. The establishment of the new multiparty governments of Ghana and Nigeria does not negate the history of failure of this political form in all parts of the continent. The idea of political freedom as practiced in the West was also a casualty of the failure of representative government. Almost all civilian regimes in Africa are one-party states and they exercise great control over the economy, the media, and what the people can do or say. Thus one should not measure success or failure of an African state on the basis of Western standards of individual freedom; rather it should be gauged by how stable the system is and whether the lives of the people have been improved by that specific government. Military regimes are normally one of the last responses to years of misgovernment by one-party states. Only the military has the potential for challenging the political leaders who condemn the usual forms of open, peaceful protest. A military regime by its nature is neither good nor bad. Some military leaders are motivated by the highest forms of patriotism while others from the very beginning use their positions for purely selfish reasons. One of the major problems inhibiting the development of even prosperous African polities has been the lack of experience of administration of senior military officers who really understand very little of the economic and political complexities of modern life. Thus the range of success of the military can range from the disaster of Idi Amin to the relatively humane, enlightened rule of Generals Ankrah and Afrifa in Ghana and al Niameiry of the Sudan. Ultimately after all discussion of commonalities has been completed, the crucial factors of political acumen and maturity depend upon a complex of local factors. The generalization, nevertheless, remains true that without proper political direction, none of the other serious problems confronting any African state can be solved.

SEVEN
Pan-Africanism, Unity, and The Cold War

Pan-Africanism as a generalized goal and specific remedy for many of the ills of the continent has enjoyed a popularity among African intellectuals and liberals throughout the world far exceeding its actual impact on Africa. Long after military coups, tribal bloodlettings, and civil and national wars have shown the centrifugal diversity of Africa, there are still intellectuals who will seriously maintain that there is a fundamental cultural and political unity operating which in time will become more apparent. Presumably if this concept is correct, evidences of this trend toward unity should be recognizable. Undoubtedly there are similarities between peoples whose languages belong to the same family, who share a generalized history, and who inhabit the same type of geographic region. However, it is difficult to see how the events of the past two decades mean anything but a shattering of the romantic version of African unity. Pan-Africanism was always a concept held by a very few of the Western educated and was used to further the cause of independence. The very act of independence and the attendant problem of building a national consensus within any African state relegated Pan-Africanism to a tertiary position on the agenda of the ruling party. Without necessarily abandoning the rhetoric connected with Pan-Africanism, politicians throughout Africa set in motion plans which negated the concept of political unification. A brief glance at the history of the Pan-African movement will show how this concept was at first a definite weapon to use against the imperialists and how later it became dangerous to African leaders attempting to develop particularistic nationalisms.

The origin of the term Pan-African is obscure, but there is no doubt that it originated with some educated person who could see common patterns in the experiences of black men in the West Indies and the United States with their brothers in Africa. One of the first users of the term was Joseph Booth, an American Baptist missionary to Nyasaland. His book *Africa for the African* as well as his practical work in southern Africa stressed that Africa was for black men and he hoped that there could be a return of those from other continents whose ancestors had been sold into slavery. Booth and his young disciple John Chilembwe helped form in 1897 the African Christian Union, one of the first organizations dedicated to African unity. Others who contributed in part to the nineteenth century dream of Pan-Africanism were the Western-educated West Africans, particularly the Fante of the Gold Coast and the Creoles of Sierra Leone.

The origins of the concept might be vague but its usage in the early twentieth century was generally precise and those who referred to the unity of Africa were easily identifiable. Some of those who wrote and dreamed of Pan-Africanism were well-educated Africans who resented their inferior status in their own country. However, by far the most active propagandists for the concept were a few West Indian and American intellectuals who mourned the separation of their ancestors from a romanticized homeland. They displayed great affection for a continent most had never seen, and longed for some type of reunion with the cultures of the black continent. Black writers, lawyers, and teachers in the United States and the West Indies saw a parallel to their inferior status and the lot of Africans living under imperial domination. Poets such as Countee Cullen and Langston Huges celebrated their kinship with Africans. Later Léopold Senghor of Senegal and Aimé Césaire from Martinique would coin the word *negritude* to express the uniqueness and importance of blackness and the cultures of Africa. The words of black writers and poets were paralleled by the actions and statements of many blacks in other professions. Men such as Dr. Edward Blyden, the West Indian-Liberian teacher and diplomat, Reverend Charles Morris, a Baptist missionary to South Africa, and Dr. Albert Thorne, a West Indian and author of an African colonization scheme are but a few examples of non-African intellectuals who concerned themselves practically and romantically with the continent. Each of these men in their own way in opposing white domination created an Africa that never existed and projected a theoretical unity based upon the non-European character of African societies and the blackness of most of the population. Very few theoreticians of early Pan-Africanism were Africans.

The man whose name is most closely associated with transferring the latent emotions of early Pan-Africanism into the realm of political action was W. E. B. Du Bois, a social scientist whose major research concern was the African heritage of black Americans. In addition to his many published works, he was one of the founders of the National Association for the Advancement of Colored People (NAACP) and was for many years the editor of its publication, *The Crisis*. In 1900 a Trinidad attorney, H. Sylvester Williams, had convened the first Pan-African Congress in London which Du Bois attended. Although little of substance was accomplished by the delegates, the meeting gave Du Bois a hint of how the disaffected black intelligencia could use such meetings as a forum for airing their grievances. The convening of the next four Pan-African Congresses was largely due to Du Bois.

The second conference was not called until after World War I. Black contributions to the Allied war effort had been substantial and Du Bois believed the time to be ripe for calling attention to the continuing wrongs suffered by blacks throughout the world. In addition the diplomats who met at Versailles in early 1919 were confronted with the problem of disposing of Germany's African empire. That the second Congress was held at all was due to the influence of Blaise Diagne, the African subminister in the Clemenceau government who was from Senegal. He persuaded Clemenceau to allow the Congress to take place despite the protests of some American and British delegates to the Peace Conference. Ultimately fifty-seven black representatives from all over the world attended. Judging from the protests of white politicians before the Congress, one would have imagined that any resolution passed would be strident and demanding. On the contrary, it was very conciliatory, very moderate, asking for international laws to protect Africans from exploitation and petitioning that the various imperial governments allow Africans to participate in government as soon as their development warranted. Nowhere was there a demand that Africans be independent of their European masters. No representatives of any major power to the Peace Conference paid any attention to the Congress and to its moderate resolution.

Du Bois and other non-Africans convened three other Congresses in the 1920s. The resolutions passed by these were similar in tone to that of the 1919 Congress. Dominated by middle-class men deeply concerned with their status but who accepted the superiority of European culture, they had faith that if their petitions were just and logically framed, the imperial powers would take steps to remedy the wrongs. This was a complete misreading of the way the governments which controlled Africa viewed their responsibilities. There were obvious economic reasons for the maintenance of an African empire which ran counter to the ideals of the early Pan-Africanists. However, the French, Belgian, and British governments believed that they had a responsibility toward the "primitive" African which in many cases transcended the desire for profits. No responsible colonial administrator in the 1920s was thinking of independence for any part of the African dependent empire. Rather, they had constructed paternalistic regimes run by Europeans but which also tried to support the traditional authorities in a particular area. That they also manipulated the chiefs and councils and in many cases misunderstood them does not remove the fact that the bulk of pre-World War II Africa was governed in partnership with African traditional rulers. Du Bois and other Pan-Africanists were petitioning European states to alter this system by shifting more authority to the Western educated by setting up governments modeled upon Europe which would, presumably, gradually take power from the European expatriate officers. It is little wonder that when colonial administrators did take note of the Congresses or the writings or speeches of men like Du Bois, they dismissed them as being the fulminations of non-Africans about a subject of which they knew next to nothing.

Africans who took part in the Congresses and who spoke out on other nationalistic issues were generally from British territories. The Belgian and Portuguese systems were too authoritarian to allow the development of an educated elite and the French whenever there was a significant number of educated as in Senegal absorbed them into the civil service. Early African nationalists were usually middle-class men who wanted not only to advance the status of Africans, but their own careers, and they were spokesmen for their class. They were dissatisfied with European rule primarily because they were denied a larger voice in governing their own lands. Early nationalists such as Joseph E. Casley-Hayford of the Gold Coast, Herbert Macaulay and J. P. Jackson of Nigeria, Edward Small of the Gambia, Harry Thuku of Kenya were at best viewed with amusement by the British authorities and at worst as potential threats to good order. At one time Macaulay was restricted to the city of Lagos. The British authorities considered him too dangerous to be allowed in the Protectorate. Thuku, a young civil servant in white-dominated Kenya, had formed in 1921 the Young Kikuyu Association to protest the hut and capitation taxes. The following year he was arrested as a danger to the peace and security of Kenya and without trial was exiled to the Northern Territories. Without his leadership the association collapsed.

'Marcus Garvey, a Jamiacan, exercised a potent influence upon black attitudes in the 1920s. He had migrated to the United States and with his charismatic personality and special message very soon developed a large following. He rejected cooperation with whites and any thoughts of ultimate integration into white-dominated societies. Thus Africa was a natural goal for Garvey and his followers. He had never been to Africa but he saw in the continent a homeland for black people from all continents. He therefore stressed a back to Africa movement which was little different in its goals from those of the white American and British philanthropists a century earlier. Garvey created a shadow government in New York, named himself Provisional President of Africa, and by means of collections from the faithful, built up a considerable economic empire. His movement never placed significant numbers of black Americans in Africa and ultimately foundered because of mismanagement of funds and the hostility of the United States and European governments. The British Colonial Office was particularly perturbed over the mischief his ideas could cause and they were primarily responsible for the Liberian government's refusal to allow Garvey to visit there. Garvey was later arrested and sentenced to prison, his movement collapsed, and he died in London in 1940 without ever being in Africa. His influence on Pan-Africanism came from his speeches and writings. This was also true of Du Bois, the Pan-African Congresses, and the few articulate African nationalists. Pan-Africanism before World War II was the concern of only a few educated Africans who followed assiduously the resolutions of the Congresses and the articles and books written by men such as Du Bois. A new generation of Africans would absorb the ideas of the earlier Pan-Africanists and use them to forge new, potent nationalist movements in post-war Africa. Kwame Nkrumah candidly admitted that Marcus Garvey had been one of the most important influences on his life.

Inspired by the activities and actions of Diagne and Du Bois, J. H. Casley-Hayford of Ghana and a few other West African intellectuals created the National Congress of British West Africa. This organization had no official standing. Its purpose was to bring together periodically West African nationalists in order to discuss common problems and to petition the British government to remedy grievances. The organization had four meetings—Accra in 1920, Freetown in 1923, Bathrust in 1925, and Lagos in 1929. In the resolutions of each they reiterated four moderate proposals. They wanted a legislative council for each British territory with at least one-half the members elected, African members of the councils to control taxation, appointment and deposition of chiefs to rest with the people, and an end to racial discrimination in the civil service. Despite the conciliatory nature of their request, the standing of the members in their territories, and the obvious weakness of the organization, their ideas were considered revolutionary by the Colonial Secretary, Lord Milner. Sir Hugh Clifford, the governor of Nigeria, no reactionary and a genuine champion of African rights, denounced the delegates to the Accra meeting as arrogating to themselves the role of spokesmen for the many dozens of West African peoples when in reality these few educated Africans had absolutely no constituency.

The last and perhaps best example of how severe imperial regimes could be when they believed any organization posed a threat was the Belgian reaction to Simon Kimbangu. The Congolese government had already in the period immediately after World War I been disturbed by the actions and theories of the Watchtower movement or *kitwala*. The *kitwala* leaders were concerned with the oppression of blacks, but taught that all would be set right by the apocalypse when all black people would be changed to white. Many of the *kitwala* followers were ready for a charismatic leader like Kimbangu, a baptised Protestant who in 1920 felt called upon to preach a version of Biblical Christianity which stressed love, charity, and equality. Very soon he had attracted a large following. Some of his more ferverent admirers claimed that Simon had performed miracles. This was too much for the Belgians who had visions of a latter day African prophet inspiring a major revolt. Kimbangu was arrested, charged with disrupting order, and in a classic case of the misuse of power, sentenced to death. In a show of magnaminity the sentence was commuted to life imprisonment. Thirty years later the prophet was still in prison in the Katanga. While incarcerated he was deified by his followers and the cult spread throughout the western Congo and into Angola. As a final repudiation of the short-sightedness of the Belgians, the church he founded, the Church of Jesus Christ on Earth by the Prophet Simon Kimbangu, with over three million members, was admitted to the World

Council of Churches in 1969. The lesson of these sordid events of the 1920s is not his final vindication, but how the imperial authorities in the interwar years could act to crush any individual or organization which seemed to threaten the peace and good order established by the Europeans.

A significant change occurred in the attitude of the European administrations in the period after 1950. No longer were they so prepared on the whisper of suspicion to bring the full weight of the police and courts to bear on African political figures. It is easy to connect this change with the growing militancy of African nationalists. However, such a conclusion is at variance with the facts. Undoubtedly a new generation of educated Africans had come to maturity during World War II and their speeches, dramas, and poetry all reflected a militancy and stridency not seen in the words of the older generation of African nationalists. Léopold Senghor celebrated in his poetry the joy of being African, Alioune Diop through his magazine *Presence Africaine* sought to educate the world with the value of African culture, and Peter Abrahams and Raphael Aramttoe attacked the warped presumptions of white supremacy.

The Sixth Pan-African Congress which met in Manchester in 1945 more than any other event marked the changed attitudes of the Western-educated elite. The Congress was a direct result of the merger in Britain in 1944 of thirteen student and political organizations to form the Pan-African Federation. Du Bois, aged 73, was invited, but the Congress was dominated by younger Africans such as H. O. Davies and S. L. Akintola of Nigeria, Jomo Kenyatta of Kenya, Joe Appiah and Kwame Nkrumah of the Gold Coast. There were delegates from elsewhere, most notably the West Indies, one of whose representatives was the ex-communist intellectual George Padmore. Most of the delegates were from British Africa and it was unmistakably a meeting controlled by Africans. The resolution of the Manchester Congress was more specific than those of the previous Pan-African meetings. It demanded the ultimate freedom of all African territory from imperial control, the creation of a system of economic democracy, and by implication rejected continued domination of African politics by traditional rulers. Instead the resolution made clear that the future of African territories should be left to the Western educated and not to chiefs and councils who had become pawns of the imperial powers.

Political scientists and African politicians have made much

of this Manchester Conference, implying a casual relationship between it and the beginnings of the devolution of political power to Africans half a decade later. There is no evidence to support such a thesis. Granted that many who attended the Manchester Congress returned to Africa and became in their own states a part of the nucleus of political activity which aided in the transference of power by the imperial authorities. The decision to allow or to suppress political activity in any African area still lay with the Europeans, and it does not appear that the British Colonial Office took more than a passing glance at the Manchester resolution. As already discussed, a variety of causes, mainly economic, caused the imperial authorities to relax their previous hard-line policy and begin instead to cooperate with the nationalists. The Gold Coast illustrates very well the confusion of the authorities during the transition from one attitude to another. Although wanting to revise the Burns Constitution, they could not at first decide whether to consider Nkrumah a menace to public safety or the leader of a respectable mass political party. Once the latter choice had been made and Nkrumah had been released from prison it was only a matter of time before the Gold Coast would gain its independence.

Nor is Nkrumah's case unique. Almost all the leading African politicians in the period immediately after World War II were watched by the European authorities to make certain that they caused no problems and a few were jailed for their statements or activities. It must have been gratifying for those in British and French territories to encounter the results of the change in attitude of the home governments. They ceased to be potential threats to the security and well-being of a state and became valued, if at times somewhat troubling, allies seeking the same goals as the European administration. The career of Felix Houphouët-Boigny mirrors the alteration of French attitudes. Viewed in the period before the 1950s as a dangerous radical associated with the communist party of the metropole, this founder of the intraterritorial *Rassemblement Democratique Africain* (RDA) was saved from prison only because he was a member of the government. Sensing the change in French policy, he modified the radical position of his party and within five years had become a valued minister in the French government and the chief architect of the seminal *Loi Cadre* which gave prime authority to the territorial councils rather than to the councils at the federal level.

The change in direction of the British and French governments should not be taken to mean that African political parties
were unimportant in the process leading to independence. They
were valuable because their formation and activities were
approved and protected by the European administrators in the
decade of the 1950s. Nkrumah, Houphouët-Boigny, Senghor,
Nyerere, and the Nigerian leaders led the way in creating mass
political parties which were destined to become the inheritors of
the imperial powers once independence had been granted. It
should be understood that these were mass parties not because the
largely illiterate populations understood and agreed with their
political objectives, but because the political leaders operating in
a favorable climate did an excellent public relations job. They
convinced the traditional African that only their political party
could achieve the economic and political goals of a specific
group. In many cases the politicians were guilty of overselling
their product—promising reforms which they knew were beyond
their powers to achieve. In some instances they lied to the people
and in others they used arguments beyond the capacity of the
people to understand but which, nevertheless, seemed to point in
the direction of something good. Such were the arguments for
Pan-Africanism which became an integral part of the drive for
independence, particularly in British territories in the 1950s.

There were two main subdivisions to the politicians' use of
the Pan-African theme during the period before independence.
One stressed the arbitrary boundaries drawn by the imperial
powers during the "scramble." They were historically accurate in
formulating this argument. The boundaries of Africa are synthetic
and arbitrary, dividing some tribes and nations into two or more
segments. These division lines had been arrived at without the
slightest concern for the African people. But many of the Western-
educated politicians went beyond this historical verity and left
the impression that once Africans again controlled the continent's
destiny, these anomalies and injustices could and would be cor-
rected.

The hope for boundary rectification rested upon the second
part of the theme which was in reality the first premise of Pan-
Africanism. That is that all black men, notwithstanding their
linguistic, cultural, and historic differences, are brothers. The
argument of the nationalists reduced to its simplest form was that
the Europeans had brought division to Africa and encouraged it in

order to maintain their control. Once independence was achieved, what could be more natural than a series of political and economic agreements between brothers which would in a very short period end the arbitrary divisions and Africa could achieve its goal of a united front against its former oppressors. To be sure, not all African politicians resorted to such a simplistic argument even during the height of the drive toward greater autonomy. Most of the French African leaders whose goals anyway were not a definite break with France shunned such rhetoric. However, many politicians in British Africa did present this argument to their followers. Among these were Kwame Nkrumah and his associates in the Gold Coast who became in the mid-1950s the symbols of success in political negotiations with an imperial power and thus an example for much of sub-Saharan Africa.

By the early 1960s both of the basic arguments for Pan-Africanism were seen by many Africans who were now the leaders of independent states as being functionally nonviable and an embarrassment to them in their major task of creating states which demanded the loyalty of all citizens. African politicians had by then learned that it is relatively easy to create a coalition of factions based on negatives. As long as the imperial power was in control, everything bad could be attributed to it. This could bring together even natural enemies who opposed the Europeans for widely separated reasons. Once a state became independent, the differences between clans, tribes, and nations began once again to manifest themselves and not even the creation of the specter of neocolonialism could impose the preindependence unity. The task of all the new governments after independence was to try to create a sense of loyalty to the state which would transcend local loyalties.

The creation of a sense of unity, so necessary in state building, was resisted by many groups within the new polities who either did not want to be a part of the new state or who believed they were not getting their fair share. The central governments reversed their previous oft stated opinions of the European-created boundaries. Instead of maintaining the logically defensible Pan-Africanist stance that these were arbitrarily imposed and should be rectified, the new governments not only accepted them, but made it clear that there would be no voluntary change in these borders. The attitude of the new political rulers makes sense taken within the context of their attempts to create a new nationalism. Holy boundaries are very important to nationalists as any student of European history can attest. However, creating such out of Africa's boundaries made nonsense of the reality of Pan-Africanism unless one wishes to follow the romantic, philosophical meanderings of the ninettenth century nationalist Mazzini who argued that nationalism must precede internationalism. The reality of nineteenth century European nationalism had already proved such speculations to be false.

Deep-seated differences between peoples banded together within a single state have caused every African leader a considerable number of sleepless nights. In some cases the result has been bloody civil war. In Burundi the Watutsi murdered the Bahutu by the thousands while in neighboring Rwanda the equation was reversed. Five years of civil war in Zaire in the early 1960s pitted Bakongo, Luba, Lunda, and dozens of other peoples against each other. The rise in power of General Idi Amin in Uganda and his later depredations must be understood within the context of tribal hatreds. The murderous long-lasting warfare between the Muslim north and Bantu south ravaged the Sudan in the 1960s and 1970s and more recently has all but destroyed Chad. The rise to power of Augustino Neto and his subsequent challengers in Angola is in part because of the differential ambitions of the Ovimbundu, Kimbundu, and Bakongo people. The list of states troubled by these internecine power struggles could be multiplied, but only one more example need be mentioned. The thirty-month-long Biafran War, put down with the cost of millions of dollars and untold thousands dead either by fighting or starvation, concerned only one major issue. This was the claim by eastern Nigerians, particularly the Ibo, that they should be allowed their independence from Nigeria.

Internal pressures generated by differing peoples within the confines of arbitrary boundaries were only one set of difficulties confronting the leaders of the newly independent African states in their attempts to obtain a national consensus. Another correlate problem related to the rectification of the borders themselves. Even before independence some groups were demanding that the boundaries be altered. The Ewe of West Africa were among the most harshly handled people when colonial boundaries were first drawn. Their traditional homeland had paralleled the coast running west to east from the eastern Gold Coast to Benin. The Ewe were divided at first into three segments dominated by the British, Germans, and French. After World War I the German dependency of Togo was divided into mandates of the League of Nations administered by Great Britain and France. Ewe politicians in the early 1950s began to campaign for Ewe unification and demanded their own state. The United Nations, Britain, and France, fully realizing the balkanization potential of such a decision, instead supported the contrary demands of those nationalists who wanted the entities of the Gold Coast, Togo, and Benin to remain unaltered. Thus Ewe nationalism was defeated because to recognize the Ewe claims would have led to constant demands by dozens of other African groups for boundary readjustments.

In the early twentieth century France had created two large administrative structures, the *Afrique Occidentale Francias* (AOF) and the *Afrique Equatorial Francais* (AEF). Each of these was administered by a governor-general. The major administrative office for the AOF was located at Dakar and for the AEF the site was Brazzaville. Each of these huge areas was subdivided into territories administered by officers who took their instructions from the governors-general. Thus, well-functioning, large unit structures were available if the French African leaders had been serious about the needs for political unity. The fact is that most of the politicians in French Africa were more concerned with economic rather than politicial consequences of Pan-Africanism. Houphouët-Boigny was of particular importance in designing the *Loi Cadre*, the enabling act of 1956, and he was not in favor of continuing the federations after independence. His reasons were largely based upon his appreciation that his state, the affluent Ivory Coast, would be required to continue to provide the funds to run the larger polity. Most of the other territories were very poor and could not provide their fair share of a recurrent budget. Other prime reasons for the breakup of the federations concerned personal ambitions of individual politicians. If the federations were broken up, opportunities to become the leader of a state would be magnified. Except for some convinced Franchophiles such as Senegal's Senghor, the bulk of French Africa's populations agreed with Houphouët-Boigny, and the federations were broken up. When independence came it was to those regions which had been subordinate territories. Political reality had triumphed over theoretical concepts of unity.

An attempt was made by some of the French African leaders to salvage some part of the unity existing in the AOF. The leading figures in this movement were Senghor of Senegal and Keita of the Soudan. Meeting with representatives of Upper Volta and Benin in December 1958 and at a follow-up conference the following month, they agreed upon federation with a central executive and legislature. Houphouët-Boigny, fearing that the Ivory Coast would lose its economic domination of Upper Volta and Benin, brought pressure to bear upon the leaders of those states to defect. They heeded the advice from the Ivory Coast and decided against the proposed union, joining instead the politically ineffective *Conseil d' la Entente* dominated by Houphouët-Boigny. Despite the change in attitude of the leaders of Benin and Upper Volta, Senghor and Keita perservered and proceeded to form the Mali Union in April 1959. Keita became by agreement the Premier and Senghor President of the Federal Assembly. The capital was to remain at Dakar. France approved the federation in December 1959, and Mali became an independent state in June 1960. By September the federation was dead, victim of different priorities in greatly dissimilar areas, lack of planning for the future, and a clash between the ambitions of Senegalese and Soudanese politicians. The constituent parts of the federation became independent states, the old territory of Soudan retaining the name Mali. Not only was political cooperation ended, but Keita closed the border with Senegal, thus blocking Mali's use of the railroad and the port of Dakar. Normal economic relations between the two states were not resumed until mid-1963.

Despite a number of attempts during the imperial period, the British were never successful in creating viable political federations. The only association of states which could have been used to establish a federation was the East African Community. In the 1920s the Colonial Office had sought to build a political federation of Kenya, Uganda, and Tanzania. This association was never completed, but there developed a number of economic accords between the three territories. These concerned common postal, rail, telegraph, air, and universities service. After independence the political leader of each state made statements which indicated that he was prepared not only to continue the economic accords, but to blend their polities together in a larger political union. Julius Nyerere, who at that time was considered by Western observers to be a near paragon of nationalist virtues, seemed particularly eager to bring this about. Domestic problems, however, occupied the attention of Nyerere, Kenyatta, and Obote when each was making these token speeches concerning unity. Obote's overthrow and Nyerere's turn toward his own version of a socialist state spelled the end not only of the hopes of political unification, but of the economic accords which defined the East

African Community. The three erstwhile partners are today much further apart than at independence. Tanzanian armed forces in a short war keyed the overthrow of President Amin of Uganda and Tanzania has closed its borders with Kenya.

One can repeat the litany of failed opportunities and border clashes, all of which show the rapid growth of feelings of national uniqueness and an eagerness to defend particularistic differences rather than advance the reality of Pan-Africanism. Surely with the belief in Pan-Africanism still strong after two decades, there must be some basis for this continuing myth. This assurance that, despite all the evidences of disunity, there is an underlying cohesiveness largely rests with the Organization of African Unity (OAU).

The OAU was born in May 1963 after the leading members of two competitve supranational organizations agreed to forget their differences and help constitute an all-embracing African organization. However, one must look briefly at the short history of these organizations to understand how compromised the OAU was even at the moment of its creation. The first supranational organization was the *Union Africaine et Malagache* (UAM) which was an outgrowth of a desire of the French African leaders to protest French policy in Algeria. This original purpose was served by a meeting in Abidjan in October 1960. Urged on by Houphouët-Boigny, the delegates decided on a further meeting at Brazzaville in December. This resulted in the creation of the *Organization Africaine et Malagache Coopération Economique* (OCAME), a purely economic organization designed to further coordinate economic policies of member states. Finally in March 1961, the charter of the UAM was signed which provided for twice a year meetings between the heads of state and the establishment of a permanent secretariat in Cotonou. In May 1961, the philosophy of the UAM was extended to non-French areas at the Monrovia Conference. Twelve of the twenty states represented at Monrovia were from the UAM.

No single person controlled the creation and direction of the early meetings. However, the philosophy of Houphouët-Boigny was pervasive for the UAM and the Monrovia group and proceeded from the established fact of the independence of the member nations. The ideal was to work toward establishing economic and political links between these polities, to find common aspirations and needs, and thus in an evolutionary fashion to seek African solidarity. Each of the African leaders at Monrovia recognized the absurdity of trying to establish some form of direct political union. From an ardent Pan-Africanist's view this was the great flaw in the UAM. Cooperation even in the economic sense being voluntary could mean a do-nothing attitude on the part of the more affluent members. The UAM was so short-lived that its impact upon Africa cannot be assessed, but it appears that Kwame Nkrumah was correct in describing it as a move away from and not toward African unity.

Kwame Nkrumah was the stormy petrel of the Pan-African movement. From the beginnings of his political campaign in the Gold Coast he stressed that independence for one state was not the ultimate goal, but a necessary step on the way to the political unification of Africa. It is difficult to know how much of his Pan-African rhetoric he believed, but in numerous speeches and all his books he championed the cause of political unification in order that Africa could be totally free from neo-imperialism. Even had he believed political unification possible during the immediate postindependence period, he must have been convinced by his own experiences that political integration was not possible once African politicians consolidated their control of their separate states. The vaunted Ghana-Guinea-Mali Union, created because Sekou Touré and Modibo Keita needed credits which Ghana could provide, was never a functioning federation. It existed only on paper and maybe in the mind of a beleaguered Nkrumah who by 1961 had become increasingly withdrawn from his own people.

Nkrumah was also the driving force behind the Casablanca Group. Formed in January 1961 in reaction to the Brazzaville meeting, it comprised a number of states with little in common except disagreement with the moderate, basic pro-West approach of the Brazzaville powers. More than half those represented during the organizational meeting were North African states. Libya, Egypt, Morocco, and the provisional Algerian government had little in common with one another and certainly their basic goals were not the same as those of Ghana, Guinea, or Mali. Very early there developed a split concerning goals between the northern polities dominated by President Gamal Nasser of Egypt and the Sub-Saharan states who followed Nkrumah. Even before the protocol establishing the group was signed in May 1961, Libya had defected and the other North African states were not supportive of Nkrumah's stand on the United Nations or the Congo crisis let alone giving up their particularistic sovreignities to further some distant Pan-African goal. The protocol did not mention political union and this should have convinced Nkrumah that his quest for immediate political unification was illusory.

Nkrumah's fervent pleas for immediate political union actually did more harm to the cause of Pan-Africanism than could have been perceived at the time. Political leaders throughout Africa who had viewed Nkrumah as a valiant leader in the struggle for African independence began to reassess him after 1960. They then saw the leader of a small independent state who wanted to expand his power base beyond Ghana. His speeches and the actions of his government labeled him as an anti-Western socialist embarked upon questionable political and economic experiments. The border crisis with Togo indicated that he was not against using raw power to intimidate weaker states. To Tafewa Balewa of Nigeria, William Tubman of Liberia, Milton Margai of Sierra Leone, as well as most French African leaders, anything that Nkrumah supported unequivocally had to be suspect. Thus their suspicions of Nkrumah's motives were added to their already considered opinion that African political union was for the present an unattainable goal.

The acquiescence of the Casablanca states in the planning for an establishment of the Organization of African Unity (OAU) in 1963 was a tacit recognition that Nkrumah's bid for a larger political complex under his direction was not possible. The many stresses placed upon the new African nations had nevertheless convinced most leaders of the need for some organization which could act to moderate differences between states, intervene in national disturbances, and prevent wars between African powers. Delegates from all African polities, with the exception of Togo, met at Addis Ababa in May 1963 and after lengthy debates produced the charter of the Organization of African Unity. Consciously modeled on the United Nations, it has a secretary general, permanent secretariat, an assembly, the council of ministers. Unique to it is the meeting of the heads of state of all member countries once a year. The responsibilities of the OAU are to maintain peace between member states, to combat neo-imperialism, and to further political and economic cooperation between African nations. It is an organization which possesses no direct coercive power itself. Thus it depends upon member states acquiescing in OAU decisions. In the decade of violence following the first major military coups, this has not been sufficient to stop the wars and civil disturbances rampant in Africa.

The OAU has been unsuccessful in ending the fighting in every major conflict where its mediation has been attempted. In Zaire, the first real test of the effectiveness of the OAU, its representatives tended to confuse rather than clarify the issues and some of its representatives were so committed to one faction that mediation was impossible. Moise Tshombe was viewed by most OAU member states as an agent of evil because of his earlier actions as head of the breakaway state of Katanga. Thus when he became prime minister and pled for OAU support to end the conflict, he was not just ignored, but villified. The OAU was also unsuccessful despite numerous attempts to end the Biafran War and the murderous series of armed clashes in Chad. The OAU as a political vehicle is successful only when the protagonists in a conflict want the intervention of a third party. Otherwise it serves the purpose of regular meetings between heads of states and other high officials, and thus it is possible that many potential conflict situations can be dealt with before they become serious. Another major role assumed by the OAU is the direction of a united front against apartheid in South Africa. The OAU here acts merely to direct feelings already approved of by each member state.

In assessing the OAU's role, a comparative ratio can be established: the OAU is to Pan-Africanism as the United Nations is to world government. While one can applaud the achievements of both, it would be foolish to assume that they play anything but a secondary role in political decision making. Both organizations arose because of the destructive tendencies of nationalism. In the Western world those have led in our century to two destructive World Wars which left in their wake 70 million dead. It was obvious in 1945 that some supranational organization was necessary to mediate between rival nationalisms. So, too, in 1963 the OAU was created to monitor the activities of the newly developed African states. However, in both institutions, sovereignty resides in the member states and not in the supranational organizations. This is far from the world of unity and harmony envisioned by Du Bois and the early Pan-Africanists. The OAU does not represent the triumph of unity, but is in reality a monument to the political divisions of Africa.

The subject of African unity cannot be closed without a brief discussion of potentially the most dangerous factor in African politics today—the intrusion of big power politics into African affairs. Kwame Nkrumah and Sekou Touré were chief among the African leaders who stridently voiced fears of a resurgence of the old imperial modes which they called neo-imperialism. While such fears are not groundless, such rhetoric tends to obscure the fact that African states could become the pawns in quarrels between non-African powers which have their genesis far from Africa. The most important has been the cold war competition for favored nation status between the United States and its Western allies and the Soviet bloc states. Recently an adjunct problem concerned with Israel has become extremely important in the politics of the Sudanic states of West Africa.

The United States traditionally has had little to do with Africa. Liberia, the only state with direct political connections to the United States, was cut adrift in the nineteenth century. American investments and trade with sub-Saharan Africa were almost nonexistent. The only exception was with South Africa where U.S. companies and investors played an important role in the development of that industrial state. However, this fact has done little to help U.S. planners since South Africa has since 1948 followed a native policy that was anathema to the various U.S. governments alert to the demands of millions of black constituents to have nothing to do with South Africa. The United States after 1960 had to put together a policy toward sub-Saharan Africa designed by career officers, very few of whom knew anything about the continent. It is not surprising that U.S. policy has been inconsistent and disjointed. Forced by political considerations at home to view the state with which it had the greatest economic ties as a pariah, it allied itself politically with states with whom it had little in common, many of whom were guilty of much greater crimes than the white regimes of southern Africa. Then, too, U.S. policy has been largely reactive. Like the dog in the manger, the State Department wanted to deny the Soviets any foothold in Africa. Without examining each case carefully, the U.S. reaction to Soviet advances has been in the main strident and generally ineffective.

Soviet policy toward Africa, although easier to understand, has also been characterized by inflexibility and stupidity. Their main long-range objective was to secure the friendship of states whose leaders claimed to be Marxists and hope that these states could be converted into satellites. Secondary objectives were to establish rights for their armed forces to use harbor, air, and other military facilities in key locations throughout the continent. As a corollary, the Soviets wanted to negate the influence of Western states, particularly in key strategic regions. Thus every time there has been a major threat to the security of an African state such as in the Sudan, Zaire, Biafra, Somalia, Ethiopia, or Angola, the Soviets have exploited the difficulties, attempting to gain long-term advantages.

This brief digression has been necessary in order to define the general roles played by both powers in Africa. In the 1950s the Soviets seemed to be making genuine progress in gaining adherents. Colonel Nasser of Egypt, Sekou Touré of Guinea, and Kwame Nkrumah of Ghana were all recipients of the Soviet's broad-handed largesse. They dutifully praised the Soviet system and damned the West for neo-imperialism. Such an apparent show of camaraderie frightened the Western press and governments into making some very silly panicked statements about Guinea or Ghana becoming the first states to succumb to communist lures. Then the Soviets, so sure of themselves, made the blunder of frightening the leaders of those African states. Jealous of their own power and not meaning to be the Soviet's cats-paw, Guinea, Ghana, and the Sudan ordered all Soviet diplomats and technicians out of their countries. Since then relations between the U.S.S.R. and these states have been normalized, but with the Soviets relegated to a tertiary position. The West, partially because of a lack of forward policy, benefited in each case from the Soviet embarrassment. Egypt represents an even more dramatic *volte face*. Once firmly believed by many to be in the Soviet orbit, it instead became increasingly pro-Western in the 1970s.

The three best examples of what cold war hostility can do to an African state are Zaire in the 1960s and the Horn of Africa and Angola in the 1970s. The revolt of the *Force Publique* soon after independence and the resultant release of old tribal animosities were disastrous for the new state of Zaire. However, the intrusion of non-African elements into the chaotic situation deepened the animosities and postponed for years a reasonable settlement of the differences. Western policy makers concluded that Patrice Lumumba was a communist and therefore, instead of supporting him as the duly elected Prime Minister, they gave encouragement to his political enemies, President Kasavubu and Moise Tshombe of Katanga. Devoid of support, abandoned by all but a few friends, and miserably protected by the United Nations forces whose help he had sought, Lumumba was murdered in January 1961 by his enemies. His death removed the one man, however weak he was, who had support throughout Zaire. It also made him a marytr and gave the communists a far better foothold in the country than otherwise would have been the case. The story which circulated throughout Africa immediately after Lumumba's death was that he was killed on orders from the United States. Communist bloc states including China supplied arms and support during the next three years to any insurgent group which would oppose the central government. One such group under the command of Christopher Gbenye made spectacular headlines in the autumn of 1964 when he took Stanleyville and his "simbas" executed over one hundred Europeans. No one can say for certain what the outcome might have been in Zaire if the great powers had not made the conflict a part of the cold war. It is probable, however, that some solution could have been reached during the first crucial months without the five years of suffering brought to the people of that unhappy state.

Two of the poorest, most backward states in Africa are Somalia and Ethiopia. However, each does have certain advantages which could perhaps be useful to the great powers. The Ethiopian highlands offer excellent positions for radar and satellite tracking stations, and the Eritrea coastline is close to the Straits of Bab el Mendeb at the southern end of the Red Sea. Somalia controls the Horn of Africa. Ships and planes based there could interdict the Red Sea, southern Arabia, and the Persian Gulf. Therefore, the cold war powers poured millions of dollars worth of sophisticated military equipment into regions barely able to feed themselves. The Soviets armed the Somalis and the United States the Ethiopians. In return, each received military concessions. Then came the 1974 coup which overthrew Haile Selassie and brought young, radical army officers to power in Ethiopia. These damned the United States for its past support of the Emperor and began to look to the Soviets for assistance. In a turnabout which would have made Machiavelli proud, the Soviets abandoned the Somalis for their newfound friends in the larger polity of Ethiopia. The United States moved into the vacuum left in Somaliland. This is not to suggest that the causes of the Somali-Ethiopian War were created by either the United States or Russia, merely that when the government of Somalia decided to take advantage of the near chaos in Ethiopia attendent on the civil war and murderous purges, they could use the most modern tanks, aircraft, and infantry weapons provided by the Soviets in order to seize the Haud and Ogaden regions from the Soviet's new ally. Despite claims to the contrary, the short, brutal little war of 1977-78, judged by military standards, was a draw.

However, the thousands of Somalis who fled from Ethiopia and are now living in relief camps in Somalia are silent witnesses to the fact that the Somalis lost. It is tempting to wonder whether, for all the belligerent irredentism of the Somali leaders, they would have chanced a major war if they had not been provided with all those clanking, shiny, new modern weapons.

Angola provides the best recent example of the confrontation of the United States and the Soviet bloc in Africa over issues primarily unconcerned with a specific African problem. The three factions to the guerrilla forces operating against the Portuguese in Angola began to fight among themselves even before independence. The most hotly contested areas were the regions around the capital, Luanda, and in the oil-producing enclave of Cabinda. Despite the support of Zaire and the United States, the FNLA forces loyal to Holden Roberto were quickly defeated by the MPLA army in Cabinda and later in the northwest sections of Angola. Augistino Neto's regular armed force was augmented by increasing numbers of Cubans who as soon as the northern front was secure were shifted southward into Ovimbundu country. It is probable that the MPLA would have won the contest with the FNLA even had they not been given Soviet or Cuban aid. Their assistance simply assured it. United States Secretary of State Henry Kissinger viewed Neto from the outset as an agent of world communism and therefore was not prepared to support his government. Instead, he decided in the crucial days before Cuban intervention to support Roberto. American aid to Roberto was arranged in a clandestine fashion and initially was not enough to offset Soviet assistance to Neto. The Congress of the United States, smarting from the Vietnamese fiasco, simply refused to underwrite Kissinger's policy and cancelled any further aid to Roberto. Whether this was done out of an appreciation of the facts of the Angolan problem or because they were tired of adventurism in foreign policy, the results were the same. The MPLA won the contest, the Cubans and Russians were firmly entrenched in northern Angola, and the United States once again bore the odium of opposing a popular government.

The civil war in Angola did not end in 1976. It still continues, only the emphasis has changed from the north to the central and southern parts of the country. Jonas Savimbi and his UNITA followers who had never accepted the legitimacy of the MPLA regime hold a major portion of the Ovimbundu territories. Despite the Cuban and Soviet equipment, the government has not even been able to reopen the critical railway linking Zaire with Benguela. There is considerable evidence that the trickle of arms and supplies reaching Savimbi have their origin in the West. In a reversal of philosophical roles, units of the South African army have penetrated into southern Angola and their air force is a constant presence near the border with Namibia. Thus the politics in Angola, like Zaire fifteen years before, have become closely tied to the competitive demands of the cold war protagonists. The MPLA government in Angola in 1981 was controlled by the Soviets and Cubans to an extent that would have shocked old-line African nationalists of the 1950s.

The preceding long and rather unfocused discourse has been necessary to touch briefly upon why the dreams of a united Africa held by the early Pan-Africanists have not been achieved. In referring to Africa, prognostication should be avoided whenever possible. However, it appears that disunity, the keynote of African political affairs today, will continue to be one of the major problems confronting the political leaders of Africa for a very long time. Acceptance of that disunity as a fact of political life may make it possible to achieve limited degrees of unity, particularly in the economic sphere. The many recent bilateral and multilateral economic agreements between African states and the creation of such organizations as the Economic Community of Westn African States (ECOWAS) indicate a growing maturity in African political life. Continuing to believe that Africa has an inherent unity based upon the skin color of the majority of its people, despite all the contrary evidence, can lead only to grossly mistaken assumptions which cloud rather than clarify the many complex issues confronting each individual African polity.

Bibliography

General

Curtin, Philip, Steven Feierman, Leonard Thompson and Jan Vansina. *African History*. Boston: Little Brown, 1978.

Davidson, Basil. *Africa in History*. New York: Macmillan, 1969.

Gailey, Harry. *History of Africa from Earliest Times to 1800*, Melbourne, Fla: Krieger, 1981.

Gailey, Harry. *History of Africa from 1800 to Present*, Melbourne, Fla: Krieger, 1981.

Hallett, Robin. *Africa Since 1875*. Ann Arbor, Mich.: University of Michigan Press, 1974.

July, Robert. *A History of the African People*. New York: Charles Scribners Sons, 1980.

Oliver, Roland, and Anthony Atmore. *Africa Since 1800*. Cambridge: Cambridge University Press, 1967.

Chapter One

GEOGRAPHIC REALITIES

Best, Alan C. G., and Harm J. de Blij. *African Survey*. New York: John Wiley, 1977.

Church, R. J. Harrison. *West Africa*. New York: John Wiley & Sons, 1963.

Clarke, John, et al. *An Advanced Geography of Africa*. Amersham Bucks: Hulton Educational Publications, 1975.

Hance, William A. *The Geography of Modern Africa*. New York: Columbia University Press, 1975.

McEvedy, Colin. *The Penguin Atlas of African History*. New York: Penguin, 1980.

Prothero, R. Mansell (ed.). *A Geography of Africa*. New York: Praeger, 1969.

Sillery, Anthony. *Africa*. New York: John Wiley, 1972.

Chapter Two

POPULATION

Brass, William, et al. *The Demography of Tropical Africa*. Princeton: Princeton University Press, 1968.

Cohen, Abner. *Custom and Politics in Urban Africa*. Berkeley: University of California Press, 1969.

Demographic Yearbooks. Lake Success: After 1948.

Elliott, Charles. *Patterns of Poverty in the Third World*. New York: Praeger, 1975.

Europa Press. *Africa South of the Sahara, 1979–80*. London: Europa Publications.

Hance, William. *Population, Migration & Urbanization in Africa*. New York: Columbia University Press, 1970.

Hanna, John, and Judith L. Hanna. *Urban Dynamics in Black Africa*. Chicago: Aldine-Atherton, 1971.

Hill, Polly. *Population, Prosperity & Poverty*. Cambridge: Cambridge University Press, 1977.

Legum, Colin (ed.). *Africa: Contemporary Period, 1972–73*. New York: Africana Press, 1973.

New Africa Yearbook, 1980. I. C. Magazines. London, 1980.

Chapter Three

ETHNIC AND CULTURAL DIVERSITY

Balandier, Georges. *Ambiguous Africa: Cultures in Collision*. London: Chatto & Windis, 1966.

Bascomb, William R., and Melville Herskovits. *Continuity and Change in African Cultures*. Chicago: University of Chicago Press, 1965.

Beattie, John. *Bunyoro, An African Kingdom*. New York: Holt, Rinehart & Winston, 1960.

Cohen, Ronald. *The Kanuri of Bornu*. New York: Holt, Rinehart & Winston, 1967.

Gibbs, James L, Jr. (ed.). *Peoples of Africa*. New York: Holt, Rinehart & Winston, 1965.

Hoagland, Edward. *African Calliope, A Journey to the Sudan*. New York: Penguin, 1979.

Hunter, Guy. *The New Societies of Tropical Africa*. New York: Praeger, 1962.

Kuper, Hilda. *The Swazi*. New York: Holt, Rinehart & Winston, 1965.

Middleton, John. *The Lugbara of Uganda*. New York: Holt, Rinehart & Wiston, 1965.

Moore, Sally, and Paul Puritt. *The Chagga and Meru of Tanzania*. Ethnographic Survey of Africa, 1977.

Morris, H. S. *The Indians in Uganda*. Chicago: Chicago University Press, 1968.

Murdock, George. *Africa, Its Peoples and Their Culture History*. New York: McGraw-Hill, 1959.

Rosberg, Carl Jr., and John Nottingham. *The Myth of Mau Mau*. New York: Meridian, 1970.

Skinner, Elliot P. (ed.). *Peoples and Cultures of Africa*. Garden City, N.Y.: Doubleday, 1973.

Trimingham, J. Spencer. *A History of Islam in West Africa*. London: Oxford University Press, 1962.

Chapter Four

AGRICULTURAL LIMITATIONS

Abercrombie, K. C. "The Transition from Subsistence to Market Agriculture in Africa South of the Sahara." E. H. Whetham and J. I. Currie (eds.), *Readings in the Applied Economics of Africa*, 2 vol. Cambridge: Cambridge University Press, 1967.

Biebuyck, Daniel. *International Africa Seminar: African Agrarian Systems*. London: International African Institute, Oxford, 1963.

Clark, Colin, and Margaret Haswell. *The Economics of Subsistence Agriculture*. London: Macmillan, 1970.

Glantz, Michael H. *The Politics of Natural Disaster, The Case of the Sahel Drought*. New York: Praeger, 1976.

Haswell, Margaret. *The Nature of Poverty*. New York: St. Martins, 1975.

Hill, Polly. *Rural Capitalism in West Africa*. Cambridge: Cambridge University Press, 1970.

Hyden, Goran. *Beyond Ujamaa in Tanzania*. Berkeley: University of California Press, 1980.

Makings, S. M. *Agricultural Problems of Developing Countries in Africa*. London: Oxford University Press, 1975.

Chapter Five

RESOURCES AND INDUSTRIAL DEVELOPMENT

Clark, W. Edmund. *Socialist Development and Public Investment in Tanzania, 1964–73*. Toronto: University of Toronto Press, 1978.

Damachi, Ukandi, and Hano Dieter Seihel. *Social Change and Economic Development in Nigeria*. New York: Praeger, 1973.

den Tuinder, Bastiaan A. *Ivory Coast, The Challenge of Success*. Baltimore: Johns Hopkins, 1978.

Jones, William I. *Planning & Economic Policy: Socialist Mali and Her Neighbors*. Washington, D.C.: Three Continent Press, 1976.

Killick, Tony. *Development Economics in Action, A Study of Economic Policies in Ghana*. New York: St. Martins Press, 1978.

Ley, Colin. *Underdevelopment in Kenya*. London: Heinemann, 1975.

Munro, J. Forbs. *Africa and The International Economy*. HC 502 in 84.

Rivkin, Arnold. *Africa and the Common Market*. Denver: University of Denver, 1966.

Tims, Wouter (Coordinating Author). *Nigeria: Options for Long-Term Development*. Baltimore: Johns Hopkins, 1974.

Chapter Six

POLITICAL STABILITY

Adam, Thomas. *Government and Politics in Africa*. New York: Random House, 1965.

Afrifa, A. A. *The Ghana Coup*. London: Frank Cass, 1966.

Austin, Dennis, and Robin Luckham. *Politicians and Soldiers in Ghana, 1966–1972*. London: Frank Cass, 1975.

Carter, Gwendolyn, and Patrick O'Meara. *South Africa: The Continuing Crisis*. Bloomington, Ind.: University of Indiana Press, 1979.

Coleman, James, and Carl Rosburg, Jr. *Political Parties and National Integration in Tropical Africa*. Berkeley: University of California Press, 1974.

Decalo, Samuel. *Coups and Army Rule in Africa*. New Haven: Yale University Press, 1976.

First, Ruth. *The Barrel of a Gun*. Baltimore: Penguin, 1972.

_____. *Power in Africa*. New York: Random House, 1970.

Gerhart, Gail M. *Black Power in South Africa*. Berkeley: University of California Press, 1978.

Gibson, Richard. *African Liberation Movements*. London: Oxford University Press, 1972.

Grundy, Kenneth. *Guerrilla Struggle in Africa*. New York: Grossman, 1971.

Gutteridge, W. F. *Military Regimes in Africa*. London: Metheun & Co., 1975.

Hailey, Lord. *An African Survey*. London: Oxford University Press, 1957.

Hatch, John C. *Africa Emergent: African Problems Since Independence*. Chicago: Regnery, 1974.

Ibingira, Grace S. *African Upheavals Since Independence*, Boulder, Co.: Westview Press, 1980.

Kirk-Greene, A. H. M. *Crisis and Conflict in Nigeria*, 2 vols. London: Oxford University Press, 1971.

Lee, Francis, and Hugh Brooks. *The Economic and Political Development of the Sudan*. Boulder, Co.: Westview Press, 1977.

Lee, John M. *African Armies and Civil Order*. New York: Praeger, 1969.

Levine, Victor. *Political Corruption: The Ghana Case*. Stanford: Hoover Institution Press, 1975.

Marcum, John. *The Angolan Revolution*, Vol. II. Cambridge, Mass.: M.I.T. Press, 1978.

Ottoway, Marina, and David Ottoway. *Ethiopia: Empire in Revolution*. New York: Africana Publishers, 1978.

Saul, John. *The State and Revolution in East Africa*. New York: Monthly Review Press, 1979.

Sherman, Richard. *Eritrea, The Unfinished Revolution*. New York: Praeger, 1980.

Staniland, Martin. *The Lions of Dagbon: Political Change in Northern Ghana*. Cambridge: Cambridge University Press, 1975.

Thompson, Leonard. *Politics in The Republic of South Africa*. Boston: Little Brown, 1966.

Welch, Claude E. Jr. (ed.). *Soldier and State*. Evanston, Ill.: Northwestern University Press, 1970.

Chapter Seven

PAN-AFRICANISM, UNITY, AND THE COLD WAR

Adelman, Kennelth. *African Realities*. New York: Crane, Russoh & Co., 1980.

Albright, David. *Communism in Africa*. Bloomington, Ind.: University of Indiana Press, 1980.

Akhurst, Frederick. *U.S. Policy Toward Africa*. New York: Praeger, 1975.

Burke, Fred G. *Africa's Quest for Order*. Englewood Cliffs, N.J.: Prentice Hall, 1964.

Cervenka, Zdenek. *The Unfinished Quest for Unity, Africa and the OAU*. New York: Africana Publishing Co., 1977.

Duignan, Peter, and L. H. Gann. *South West Africa—Namibia*. New York: Americana Affairs Association, 1975.

Gibson, Richard. *African Liberation Movements*. New York: Oxford University Press, 1972.

Kitchen, Helen. *Africa from Mystery to Maze*. Lexington, Mass.: D.C. Heath, 1976.

Legum, Colin. *Pan Africanism*. New York: Praeger, 1965.

Nyerere, Julius. *Freedom and Unity*. Dar es Salaam: Oxford University Press, 1966.

Padmore, George. *Pan Africanism or Communism*. New York: Doubleday, 1970.

Sithole, N. *African Nationalism*. London: Oxford University Press, 1969.

Thompson, Vincent B. *Africa and Unity*. New York: Humanities Press, 1970.

Touval, Saada. *The Boundary Policies of Independent Africa*. Cambridge, Mass.: Harvard University Press, 1972.

Woronoff, Jon. *Organizing African Unity*. Metuchen, N.J.: Scarecrow Press, 1970.